JOSE MARTI
Versos Sencillos

JOSE MARTI
Versos Sencillos

F64 Books
F64 Books / F64 Pro
9903 Santa Monica Blvd, Suite 647
Beverly Hills, CA 90212

Copyright © 2023 by Riley Perez

FIRST TRADE PAPERBACK ORIGINAL EDITION

All rights reserved, including the right to reproduce this book or portions thereof in any form whatsoever, including but not limited to print, audio, and electronic. For more information, address:
F64 Books/Riley Perez
9903 Santa Monica Blvd, Suite 647
Beverly Hills, CA 90212.

Set in Times New Roman
Printed in the United States

10 9 8 7 6 5 4 3 2 1

Publisher's Cataloging-in-Publication data
Names: Riley Perez, author.
Title: Jose Marti: Versos Sencillos / Riley Perez.
Description: First Trade Paperback Original Edition / F64 Books
New York, NY; Los Angeles, CA: F64 Books, 2023
Identifiers: ISBN 978-1-7372340-9-8
Subjects: Marti, Jose / Perez, Riley / Prisoners-Cuba-Cuba-biography. / Prisons-Cuba-Havana-Anecdotes. / History of Cuba-Cuba-Anecdotes. / Bank robbery. / Cuban Stories & Cuban Experience / Political Prisoners & Political Refugees.
Editor: Conti, Peter / Book Design: Ferendo, Frank
Artist, Kar, Ida(1964) ©National Portrait Gallery, London

"Life inevitably translates into time. That is why the sum total of it is called 'a lifetime'. Freedom is the potential to spend one's time in any fashion one determines. I would always want the time invested in my ideas to be profitable, to give the reader something lasting for their investment in me. It is very important to me that my ideas be understood. It is not as important that I be understood. I believe that this is a matter of respect; your most significant asset is your time and your commitment to invest a portion of it considering my ideas means it is worth a sincere attempt on my part to transmit the essence of the idea. If you are looking, I want to make sure that there is something here for you to find."
— Gil Scott-Heron

Contents

Editor's Note	9
Prologue	14
Jose Marti	17
Client #5	33
Tick-Tockers	43
Emotions	50
The Pitch	53
Room 104	70
Georgie Porgie	88
A Cow, A Cat & A Horse	108
TRIMALCHIO IN WEST EGG	112

The characters originally appeared in F. Scott Fitzgerald's *The Great Gatsby*

DISPATCH FROM THE FRONT LINE:	119
Not Today Opie & AVISO! SIN AVISO!	
Acknowledgements	128

Editor's Note

In 2003, Riley Perez was living in James Epstein's guesthouse. For inspiration while writing his first screenplay, Riley would sit in James's father's chair – the same chair that the elder Epstein, wrote the classic *Casablanca* screenplay in with his twin brother, Phillip G. Epstein. Riley's chips were stacked; the streets were nearly in his rear window. He was finally ready to embark on his writing career.

Then he got a call. Against his better judgement, Riley took the job, more as a favor to an old friend than anything else. That job ended up costing him ten years of his life.

While Riley was incarcerated, he didn't do much writing, but instead, stored his experiences in his head. When he was released, he set a regimented schedule out of his waterfront apartment in Marina Del Rey, where he spent his days writing – the waves and sunshine, a stark contrast to his dreary cell. Two years later, *What Is Real? The Life and Crimes of Darnell Riley* was published. I had the honor of introducing Riley at his first ever public reading, which was held at Diesel Bookstore in Brentwood. A diverse crowd, which packed the courtyard, was a testament to Riley's background. Growing up Cuban in Koreatown and the Hancock Park sections of Los Angeles, Riley has been able to traverse multiple socioeconomic, ethnic, and racial landscapes. His audience was a testament to that.

What is Real? stays away from the cliches of life in a penitentiary, instead, it focuses on the psychological and sociological aspects of prison. It reminded me of one of my favorite TV shows, *The Wire*. Riley's book, like the beloved series, is a slow burn that digs deeply into the fabric of crime and punishment, highlighting how one's incarceration not only affects the inmate, but also how it reverberates through his family and friends. It shies away from rah-rah over the top violence and spectacle. When tragedy strikes, the reader feels it, like a slow knife penetrating skin and guts, as opposed to a fuselage of bullets. I was deeply moved by Riley's tome, and I have taught it several times in my college writing classes at CUNY and Columbia.

For the last five years I have watched Riley grow as a writer and a human. Whether working on his screenplays, documentaries, or in the writers' room for the hit CBS show *Fire Country*, Riley has displayed a work ethic and drive that is rare these days.

About a year and a half ago, Riley mentioned he was writing a collection of short stories. Unlike when most of my "writer" friends who say they are going to write something but seldom get beyond the treatment stage, I actually believed him. Sure enough, a year later, he showed me the manuscript for *JOSE MARTI: Versos Sencillos,* and I was blown away.

Riley's prose is at once timely and artistic. His writing flows smoothly but one can quickly ascertain that a great deal of effort went into the words. In fact, it reminds me of the writing of one of Riley's literary heroes, F. Scott Fitzgerald. It may be easy to read, but the reader knows he is reading literature. Take this excerpt from the jewel of the collection, "Jose Marti," where the title character is discussing his father's lineage:

> Mi papa, Jorge Luis Martí, was a mulato prieto. His father's African and Taino blood was stronger than his mother's Spanish heritage. The confluence of the two

> bloods gave him the appearance of a strong Romanesque face that belonged on a coin. The thick locks that fell over his dark skin made him look like a fierce warrior in constant battle with the elements. His manner of speech was influenced by his time in exile where in Mexico he served as a guard to Fidel Castro.

When I read Riley's writing, it transports me back to a time when authors took their time to construct a narrative. That's not to say that Riley's stories are in any way old-fashioned. Quite to the contrary. They tackle situations that look like they're ripped from the headlines: a drunk girl almost drowning in Malibu; a court that punishes those who are not woke enough; a reunion of Beverly Hills High School alumni; a reimagining of *The Great Gatsby*; and a few barber shop jokes. Side note: Riley used my old apartment as a setting for a low-class call girl; I'm proud to say I have since moved from that questionable docile.

One of my favorite exercises is to juxtapose "Jose Marti" with the other stories in the collection. Even though it is a contemporary piece like the others, the difference is profound. My knowledge of Cuba is limited.

After reading "Jose Marti" I feel that I finally have a sense of the desperation and yearning to escape – not so different than life in prison.

I am honored to have edited Riley's collection of short stories.

Peter Conti
6/17/23
Los Angeles

Prologue

I don't think that this book is for anyone born after 1988. Why '88 and not '87? Well, did you ever drink out of a water hose while playing outside for hours? Are you old enough to have watched the first season of *America's Most Wanted* and from the show, understood why as a kid you shouldn't talk to sketchy dudes in serial killer type of vans, but you still did it anyways because your ragtag crew courted danger as part of a rite of passage?
Well, if the potential of being abducted by a serial killer didn't scare you off, then you should be okay with this collection of stories. I put them together during the global pandemic. In between the daily updates on the efficacy of wearing mask, covering your body with Purell disinfectant or standing six feet apart from the person in front and behind you in the supermarket, I managed to peck on the ole finger pecker and arraigned some simple words into simple verses that hopefully, unlike the many volumes of pandemic mandates that the world was subjected to, these stories won't be debunked and tossed into the dustbin.

They may cause you to laugh, just as the innocent neighbor – possible seral killer - laughed as he looked at the alley apples that we used to destroy his serial killer style van. He saw it proper that the existential threat of living in proximity to a serial killer and taking action was something that he would've done as a kid. Granted, our parents had to pay for the repairs and in return, we were able to hang out with a Vietnam veteran who taught us how to give cars a tune-up, from oil change to spark plug switch-out. He taught us how to sharpen knives and how to have the proper measurement when he was casting his own bullets. We didn't see danger in that or in the neighbor allowing us to use his .22 rifle to test the bullets that he made (under his watchful eye at the LA River).

Hanging out with the odd neighbor got us to lower our guard and accept that he wasn't a serial killer, just a man from another era who lived as he saw fit. He had a ferocious looking pitbull that we won over with treats, a ferret that lived in the van that doubled as his workstation, complete with the tools needed as a locksmith - or maybe that was his well-crafted cover, and he was a serial killer.

None of us were abducted and the guy moved on to Northern California. There was no internet at our fingertips to find out if there was an uptick in abductions in the town he moved to, so all we had was *Americas Most Wanted* on Saturday night.

If the shorts cause you to consider a position that you've taken and adjust or if you just laugh at the absurdity that comes with being middle-aged and not taking yourself and trends too seriously, then I will have done my job. If I end up cancelled from any of the stories, then I've still done my job. Go ahead, break out your knives or prepare a belly laugh.

Tracie & Azline, forever in my thoughts.

JOSE MARTI
Versos Sencillos

30 de mayo 2021

    ¡Acere, que bola! I am Jose Enrique Batista-Marti. From birth, I was blessed with strong lungs and a heart that beats like a rabbit. Mi mama, Azline Batista, reminded me as a baby that my eyes and heartbeat were coordinating like sentinels on guard as I surveilled the world around me. If I identified something or someone in a room, my heart would slow to a stop as my eyes focused on the object, with my heart resuming its conga thudding once my eyes accepted the object as being pleasing, which gave way to my smile. This is not my attempt to convince you that I have extra sensory skills, or that at an early age I had a gift of charm, it is simply the tale that was repeated to me.

    Mi cumpleanos es el 14 de mayo de 1977 and as I write this story, I have survived 44 years of life. Mi mama, Azline, bears the name of her father, Fulgencio Batista, the ninth president of Cuba. Her birth was the result of Senor Batista's sudden divorce from his first wife, Elisa Gomez for mi abuela, Marta Fernandez Miranda, who had served as one of his many mistresses, but the only one that he acknowledge by marrying so that their children would not be bastards.

    Mi abuela was born in Cuba to Jewish parents whose family had lived on the island going back to the early 1800s. They had extended family in Spain whom they sponsored to come to Cuba at times, so her union with Senor Batista raised the family name and provided support for the Jewish community in Cuba, as many didn't see the need to flee the island for La Yuma.

    Senor Batista was the first and only non-white Cuban to rise to the presidency. Although he presented as a mulato blanco, he was the product of Spanish, African, Chinese and Taino ancestry, and for that, my mother and her many siblings resembled and advertisement for the United Nations.

Mi papa, Jorge Luis Marti, was a mulato prieto. His father's African and Taino blood was stronger than his mother's Spanish heritage. The confluence of the two bloods gave him the appearance of a strong Romanesque face that belonged on a coin. The thick locks that fell over his dark skin made him look like a fierce warrior in constant battle with the elements. His manner of speech was influenced by his time in exile where in Mexico he served as a guard to Fidel Castro.

Jorge Luis Marti stands in the history books as a champion of the Cuban motto, "Patria o Muerte". It is with that spirit that mi papa decided to leave his comfortable government position and to return to the field as a military liaison for the Grenada government in 1983. He was 55 years old, and as he had said to me when discussing the defense of our homeland, "todos os dias despues del 26 de Julio es un regalo." I understood the opposition that his vanguard faced when on the 26th of July 1953: they attacked the army barracks at Santiago to overthrow the Batista regime. To him, every conflict he faced after did not compare to that experience, and every day that he lived since was a gift, borrowed time, because he had already passed the expiration date for a revolutionary.

My parents came from two separate families in Cuba: One was Batista, the dictators who curried favor with La Yuma and opened the gates to industries. The other, was the opposition whose stated goal was to ensure that the affairs of Cuba were to the benefit of Cubans and not the government to the north.

The success of mi papa's side ushered in the leadership of the Castro brothers. For mi mama, Senor Batista fled for Portugal and her family fortune fled with him. She was already of legal age and working in her uncle's sugar processing company and was unable to return to Havana. From that day on, she assumed the surname Miranda, from her mother.

My parents knew of their respective lineage but agreed they would not speak of it in public, as it was understood that his position in the Castro's inner circle would be negatively impacted if it was revealed that a Batista was in their midst. Their dedication to one another and a united Cuba is what influenced their decision to name me, Jose Marti, after the one figure in Cuba that all sides in the political divide accept as the voice of the Cuban people. Jose Marti was the poet whose writings all Cubans have drawn from as a driving force in the pledge of Patria o Muerte. That pledge influenced Fidel Castro as he cited Jose Marti as the intellectual author of the 26 de Julio attack. That pledge convinced the judges to spare his life as Castro served as his own counsel where he waxed poetically that the offenses that he was accused of "organizing an uprising of armed person against the Constitutional Powers of the State" was incorrect, for he and his guerilla army of patriots had revolted against Batista. Castro was successful. Mi mama's family was not.

Mi papa's decision to serve in Grenada was precipitated by mi mama's decision to leave Cuba in the 1980 Mariel boatlift. She did not consult anyone. She decided to leave, like many, and has not returned to the island, "ella vive en la Yuma." Mi papa would spit every time that he acknowledged her flight from the homeland.

Mi papa was living on the island of Grenada, overseeing the construction of a new airport runway. La Yuma's president, Ronald Regan knew that it was not a runway for commercial purposes as the island's growing tourist industry needed. The length and width could accommodate Russian military planes, and President Regan could not allow this in his backyard. The leaders of Jamaica, Dominica, Antiqua and Barbados, and the Grenadian opposition forces agreed and in October of 1983, without the approval of the UN Security Council, La Yuma invaded. Mi Papa was one of two Cuban soldiers who were killed, leaving me an orphan.

Because of mi papas service to Cuba, I was treated with respect. Mi papa's family raised me, and once I completed my university studies in Economics, I donned the military uniform for the prescribed time of service and swore to the tradition that every Cuban is a citizen soldier.

At 18, I was set to compete in the 1996 Olympic Games in the sport of fencing, but months prior, I was working a construction project at the port of Havana when a crane that was offloading supplies collapsed, causing the cargo to crash onto the pedestrian walkway where I was standing. When I woke up in the hospital, I was encased like a Bratwurst. I had sustained breaks in my left femur, but I was alive.

Roland Tucker filled my place on the team in the foil competition and won a bronze medal. Days before the games had started, mi hermano, the boxer Joel Cassamoyor and his teammate Ramon Garbey, fled to Mexico. For that the entire Cuban delegation was confined to quarters in Albany, Georgia as the games were being held in Atlanta, yet the desire to live free had already infected another Cuban athlete, Rolando Arrojo. Rolando saw his opportunity and left the teams lodging to the open arms of La Yuma where he was granted asylum. Had I not been staring at my mangled leg; I too would've taken the opportunity.

Once I was ambulatory, I was offered a position with the Transval company. Although Transval is presented as an example of private enterprise thriving in Cuba, it is just like every other social program on the island—propaganda. Because of my military service and lineage and my university education that included my command of the English language, I was assigned as Commander of Logistics. Transval's reach stretched into several sectors, but the focus for the government permitting the company to exist is for the collection of foreign currency.

Since the 2016 visit by President Barack Obama to Cuba, where he announced the easing of travel restrictions, Cuba has seen an influx of tourists from La Yuma. With the tourists comes the opportunity for commerce and the Castro's want to control who spends what and where, and for that, the Castro's system of permissible currency only allowed for Cubans to have in their possession the Cuban or the Convertible Pesos for daily use. Unlike the Convertible Peso, which can be exchanged in other Latin-American countries, the Cuban Pesos can only be used in Cuba. If an individual provides a service, one can accept payment in the form of the Euro or British pound but must immediately seek to convert it to one of the two pesos. The currency of La Yuma may be the preferred currency of exchange throughout the world, but in Cuba, it can lead to imprisonment if one is caught hoarding, even for sentimental reasons.

At Transval, my focus was to take possession of foreign currency and deliver it to the Treasury Office of Foreign Assets. My station at Transval was not one that an ordinary Cuban can achieve. I had been given this duty because of mi papa's service to the Castro's and because I was unable to attend the Olympic Games in La Yuma, I did not defect.

Daily, I had up to nine patrols of armored guards in teams of two collecting foreign currency from hotels, restaurants, bars, and any foreign embassy that sought to engage in a commercial transaction throughout Habana. Several years ago, I was allowed to bring on mi hermano, Alexander Hoang-Perez. In the true tradition of the mulatto experience, Alexander, or "Kiki," as we called him, was the product of the Chinese that came to Cuba as indentured servants on his mother's side. They mixed with the Spaniards of the noble class. On his father's side, his name Alexander honored his father's Soviet blood. No matter the family origin, they have all honored Patria o Muerte. They were Cuban.

Kiki's Oriental eyes and milky Russian skin have survived many hot Cuban days. Kiki followed me into the military and stayed, further cementing his dedication to the defense of the homeland. When I requested Kiki to be my right hand, the government didn't resist.

The highlight of my Friday pick-up was our last two stops. The Hotel Saratoga, the spot where wealthy foreigners and dignitaries frequented when visiting the island. The Saratoga is where my wife Margara worked as the general manager. It was a bonus knowing that she had a cup of Café Cubano and cookies waiting for us. Kiki flirted with the tourists as Margara arranged the currency in stacks based on the level of sensitivity, with bills from La Yuma in a separate stack, sealed in a government issued plastic case that she deposits into a lockbox for me to add to my satchel.

Once I finished my café, I pleaded for a kiss. She relented only after she was sure no one could see. We end our embrace with me humming the words of Jose Marti: "Guantanamera. Guajira Guantanamera. She is all I have. The short girl with the big eyes and inviting lips." No matter how much time had passed, she reminded me of the pitiful thing I said to her on the last of countless attempts of mine to get her attention. I had just recovered from my accident and was starting at Transval. Margara was new at The Saratoga, and as she walked past me, as she had done many times before, not realizing that my internal voice was audible I said, "un madre asi. Por que un nino necesitaria juguetes?" It was juvenile, but she understood it was not my intention to offend, only wanting to voice my pleasure when viewing her perfectly shaped, oscillating hemispheres that trailed behind her as she passed, but it worked.

The next stop after the Saratoga was to the Partagas Cigar Factory where Juan Ramos oversaw the assembly and distribution of one of the crown jewels in the Cuban cigar industry. Tourists were permitted inside to watch Torcedors work their craft, and from the moment they entered the building, the visual cues that you have entered a government operation were evident in the life-size photographs of the Castro's, Che Guevara and other figures of The Revolution that graced the walls on every floor. Surveillance cameras and government appointed inspectors surveilled the building singling out any tourists that ignored the warning upon entry to check in their cameras with the security, another cue that made it clear the government wants to control every aspect of your experience, which extends to state-approved photographs of the factory, which were sold as the tour finished.

Juan also served with Kiki and me in the military. Where I stand 5'9" and have added 30 pounds to my frame since service, Juan's 6'3" hulking figure had been with him since he was a teenager. He was a mulatto blanco, with the face that resembles the clenched fist of a gorilla. The idea that he could be considered attractive to a woman had never been a thought that has touched his ego, in part because he had been committed to his childhood lover, Mayuri.

Kiki and I entered the factory from the loading dock to avoid the line of tourists who had jockeyed to enter the building. Juan ushered us into his office where he had prepared the foreign currency in order of importance, and just like at the Saratoga, the currency from La Yuma is sealed in a plastic case and placed in a lockbox. Unlike at our stop with Margara at the Saratoga, Juan prepared several boxes of cigars for us to take as we left the building. The only way for us not to be seen by the camera that overlooked the loading dock was by Juan standing in front of it, blocking the government's view of us walking out with cigars valued at 12,000 pesos.

Juan's primo Esteban, a little wiry guy, waited for us a block away from the factory. We handed him the boxes that he turned around and sold to tourists at the international hotels. Pilfered Partagas cigars sold at discounted rates was one of many items that Esteban sold in the black market to tourists. His preferred form of payment to tourists from La Yuma that return to Cuba was for them to provide him with information. Every time that he told a tourist he wanted information, they were shocked at what exactly he meant, until he spelled it out: "Bring me four memory cards; one with as many Hollywood movies that can fit on it; one with as many Hollywood television shows, but be sure to have *Seinfeld*, the show *Lost*, and Jay Leno, one with music videos from every genre of music, and the last one full of news."

Information was currency in Cuba. The Castro's controlled what information we could consume, so for Esteban to have access to the memory cards meant he would be able to place Hollywood films, television shows, videos, and news information onto individual memory cards that he could sell. This was Cuba, where we interacted with tourists who seemed as if they had been punched into a coma by Juan's massive paws when they heard that information was of the highest order on the black market.

Juan and Esteban would travel on our weekly Friday pilgrimage to the Pinar del Rio region where Juan's adoptive family, the Montesino's, tended to their tobacco farm, Finca Montesino, as they have done for five generations. The plan for the night was to finalize our most audacious venture.

I usually arrived home before Margara, but on this day, she was waiting for me in the living room of our Soviet Brutalism-designed apartment in the Miramar district of Habana, a mere two blocks from the Russian embassy. Our neighbors were all foreign dignitaries and soon after we moved in, the ambassador to Venezuela invited us for dinner. If the news reports we saw on the information that Esteban circulated was true, then the citizenry of Caracas would not approve of the indulgent meals the ambassador's family enjoyed, as the countries rationing drove them to eat pigeons and scavenge through rubbish for meals.

The apartment was a gift of sorts from the government to ingratiate my family into The Revolution, an act that was seen as the final step before

I was asked to join the government in an official capacity, which was made public, marking me as communist in the history books.

Before I could adjust to Margara's tear-filled eyes, she let her excitement spill out, "estoy embrazada!" We were going to have a child, something that had eluded us for years, not for lack of practice, it just hadn't been our time.

*****

Filled with joy, I did not realize I was smiling as I drove down the Malecon in our 1977 Lada. The automobile had belonged to my parents. In a 40-year span of time, I went from sitting in the backseat to manning the wheel with a cigar in hand as mi papa did as he drove around Habana. Not much maintenance was required as the machine was simply constructed. "Just add petroleum and it may run forever" should've been the advertisement for the automobile. Like any automobile that came to the island, once it arrived, the law stated that it could never leave. Leaving… that thought lingered my mind constantly back then.

On a Friday night, the Malecon was filled with activity. Lovers lounged on the concrete sofa that was eight kilometers in length; music was projected from automobiles and impromptu bands, who set up throughout the esplanade, showcasing their talents. When I saw a section empty, I guided the Lada to the side of the road. Before Margara could object to my maneuver, I ran to her door, opened it and took her hand, guiding her to an area where I brushed the concrete so she could sit as I faced her. Habana Harbor was in the background.

Margara pestered me to find out why we had stopped on the esplanade. "Nos vamos a los estados Unidos," I said, shocking Maragara, who was unable to speak. "Our baby can be born in the US," I added.

Seconds went by before she said, "Why tell me here?" I didn't know if her question was a yes or no answer or if it was her ploy to gain more information so she could turn me over to the government. Maybe she was liking her new Venezuelan neighbors and the favors that are conferred on officials in the government. Maybe I had errored in telling her that was all I could think, but then she hugged me and whispered, "Yes. To La Yuma. We will go Disneyland, the Grand Canyon, Niagara Falls. I want to see it all with you." I was saved. I had all that I would need to make the journey.

Before we walked back to the Lada, I instructed Margara not to discuss our flight with anyone, and that we would only discuss our plans at the Montesino farm with Juan, Kiki, Esteban and Mayuri who would accompany us to La Yuma. I did not have to repeat my instructions—something every Cuban understands—that neighbors, coworkers and family members can sell information to the government for the reward of extra tarjetas or preferential job placements. In addition to informants, other surveillance measures could be in place where our apartment or automobile could be wired, considering that I was soon to be accepted into the ranks of the party.

The remainder of the drive to the farm was spent enjoying the view of the countryside with the sound of 80s British rock n' roll playing. Margara sang along at the top of her lungs to the Pet Shop Boys's "West End Girls", Duran Duran's "Rio", and Depeche Mode's "Master and Servant". We had every hit song of that era that Esteban was able to fit onto a CD, and they all spoke of an era that those of us in Cuba associate with the changing of the guard, the fall of communism when the Berlin Wall came down. It was a fitting selection considering the journey that we had ahead.

One last look at old Habana was marked by the last of a row of billboards that tell the tale of an oppressed people. There was an image of a noose, with the words "BLOQUE" in bold letters. Margara looked at the many European tourists that drove next to us in 1950s automobiles and we laughed, knowing that the Castro's propaganda campaign was on its final leg.

Once at dinner, Margara didn't let on to anyone that she was aware of our plan. I had told her that we only discuss the flight while walking the fields at the farm. So, when the four of us stood and unholstered our cigars, the Montesino family knew that we were going for our walk, and that we had moved from plotting to the action stage as Margara and Mayuri accompanied us.

The farm provided much comfort and security for what we were discussing. We had refuge with the Montesino's as they had suffered a great deal under the Castro's rule. For five generations, the family had been good shepherds of the land, which is situated in the lush Penar del Rio are of Cuba. The region's tropical climate provided a hospitable climate for the tobacco farmers that knew what the changing of the clouds meant for their crops. The farmer mentality remained with the Montesino's. It was a family tradition that they are preserving as they rose before the sun and worked at a labor-intensive profession. They've served as hosts to the Castro's at the beginning of The Revolution only to witness the Castro's imposition of a series of laws that appropriated large parts of their land to the state. The first in the agrarian land grab was sold to give land to the workers by not allowing farms to be more than 402 hectares. When the Castro's no longer cared about the narrative, they reduced ownership of farmland to 67 hectares. Tobacco farmers were then mandated to sell 90% of their production to the state at the state's price, only allowing the farmers to sell the remaining 10% on the open market, with a hefty tax for produce leaving Cuba.

Once at a safe distance in the fields, we exchanged handshakes and hugs as Margara and Mayuri wiped tears from their eyes, which signaled for me the time was ripe to go through the order of flight.

"Friday at 3 p.m., Esteban will be in the main viewing area of the Museo de la Revolucion," I said. Without a second of dead are, Esteban added, "I will already have spread the word throughout the afternoon that the treasures are fake, propaganda and that we are demanding that patriots come view for themselves." Juan added, "Encourage, do not demand. If they are patriots then you will not have to demand, they will want to see for themselves, the suggestion will pique their curiosity," Esteban agreed.

Juan continued, "I will have the lancha at the harbor filled with petroleum and rations. I've secured a handheld Marine GPS unit." Kiki asked, "Do you have backup batteries?" Firm in his response, Juan looked off in the distance as he released a plume of smoke from the cigar that he cradled with his massive lips, "he sonado con esas 90 millas a la libertad, I know it intimately."

Satisfied with his answer, Kiki added, "At 3 p.m., me and Jose will leave the factory. We will have the packages with us. Jose is driving while I separate it all in the back of the van." Estaban released a sinister grin then added, "by 3:05pm, I will begin breaking cases and slicing at textiles."

Hearing the plan for the first time, Margara and Mayuri's shocked faces informed us that the simplicity of our plan had not been considered by ordinary citizens, which meant that if we executed it correctly, the government would not be aware until we are far into La Yuma's waters.

Mayuri asked, "Por que estas destrozando el museo?" Esteban answered, "It is a distraction. The treasures that are on display are fake. Propaganda that the government sells to us that our nation's treasures are for the nation to enjoy. If everyone saw that they have lied to us about that, then maybe we have been lied to about other things. Where are your father and brother? They have not stood before a judge. It has been two years, and there has been no trial." Mayuri nodded in agreement. Then Margara asked, "What is in the package that you two will have in the van?" I watched as Esteban, Juan and Kiki chuckled and then added, "Euros, British Pounds and the preferred currency of the world, the US dollar. We are taking the money."

*****

The next week was an exercise in playing theatre. We all agreed to continue to play the characters we were known to be, characters that we knew intimately: Kiki and I were civil servants; Margara and Mayuri worked in hospitality and were a part of the propaganda machine that was presented to the tourists—a private industry was thriving on the island; Esteban maintained his role as the de facto powerbroker of the black market where he procured for families and government officials alike a variety of entertainment outlets. We just had to get to Friday without adjusting our characters. We just had to be ourselves.

My salary allowed for a few creature comforts, but over the years I had made it a priority to take Margara to a restaurant at least once a month. After paying rent and ensuring that the refrigerator shelves were full there weren't many pesos left to enjoy a night out in the town, which is where the pilfered cigar racket came in. Consistently, we each took in half of our salary with the sale of the cigars to the tourists. Margara got finder fees from Esteban whenever she referred tourists to him that were looking to get into El Gato de un Ojo, preferential treatment at Bodeguita del medio and for those that wanted the experience of being in the presence of the Superman of Habana, whose appendix had been liken to the length and girth of the battle-tested cannons that guard the ports of Habana.

In the tradition of keeping up with our routine, we hiked the marbled steps of the spiraling staircase into the Paladar La Guardia, passing the long hallways that house multi-generational families who had occupied the building that was once known as La Mansion Camaguey. Once inside, the host Deyanira, a former Olympic volleyball player who had maintained her athletic physique, greeted us with an embrace. Because of the rumors that she was a lesbian, the government censured all of her interviews when traveling internationally, so when she opted to hold onto Margara's arm as she guided us to our table on the terrace, I looked for signs that she had carnal interest in my Margara. If out of interest in currying favor with Margara, or possibly because of the rumors of me joining ranks in the government, we were given a table that overlooked the bustling neighborhood where children and seasoned street vendors jockeyed for the attention of tourists, as they peddled their wares. Our waitress tended to us as if we were the only patrons in the restaurant.

The city of Habana was in the midst of a red meat shortage but the chefs at La Guardia had planned ahead and purchased other restaurants' meat supply at inflated prices. They knew they wouldn't make much profit, but they never wanted to be without a variety for their patrons to enjoy.

Margara stuck to the instructions of not discussing our flight anywhere but at the farm. I knew that she wanted to talk of all of the experiences that awaited. Her constant smile and far-off stares at parts of the city that had been home to her informed me that she understood that once we left, we could never return, that is, if the Castro's were still in power. And if history was an indicator, they would always be in power.

*****

2:45 p.m. Kiki and I exited the Saratoga Hotel. We exchanged head nods with Margara and Mayuri who knew that it was then time for them to leave and head to the harbor where Juan would be waiting.

I stood guard as Kiki entered the armored van where he made his way to the secured area and began separating the packages of currency. We agreed that all the Cuban and Convertible Pesos would be given to the harbor master for allowing us to borrow his boat. Once he had time to count the pesos, he would realize that our use of the word "borrow" really meant that he had just sold us the boat.

I maneuvered the van through heavier than normal traffic and eventually decided to take alternate turns to ensure that we got in and out of the Partagas factory in less than five minutes for us to maintain our timeline.

3:00 p.m. The sweat dribbled down Kiki's face as he unloaded the currency from the factory with the precision of a casino croupier. His nerves were steady. We knew once we decided to turn left instead of going right onto Paseo del Prado that we had sealed our fates and there was no turning back. There would be no more inspections of currency over small talk with government officials at the Treasury Office of Foreign Assets. I was driving when we had crossed the rubicon.

3:05 p.m. Esteban had already gathered a crowd of agitators at the museum. Most of the onlookers in the crowd where artists from outside of Habana who often found themselves in the crosshairs of the government for political stunts that they carried out in the attempt to gain attention to their art and hopefully drive up the price.

Once Esteban began smashing vases and slashing textiles with his cuchillo, most of the crowd fled as they realized that the security had been alerted. Esteban having done his job, then made his way to the harbor where he saw Juan and Mayuri waiting.

Moments later, Kiki and I arrived. "Que te pasa Esteban?" Kiki barked out in frustration. "No one cared. Forget it. We are here now" was all Esteban could reply, and it was true, we were present, except Margara. I looked to Juan, who by then was gritting his teeth as he helped Kiki and Esteban load the satchels of currency onto the boat. Mayuri spoke through her tears, "ella se fue a casa."

I thought of how we all agreed we would continue to play the characters we had been playing for all our lives up to this point, but never did I think Margara had assumed another character all together - I had never known her to be a coward. Before I could decide what to do next, Mayuri added, "algo ha pasado." It was obvious something had happened to her and whatever it was, I had to be with her. I could not leave her alone to be persecuted for being a conspirator in my plot to flee.

I embraced Esteban, Kiki, Juan and Mayuri with a hug. I did not have to push them away, as we all agreed if anyone was captured or decided to exit the plot then the others were free to leave without guilt. I stood at the Habana Harbor as the lancha sped away until the distance between us had reduced their image to the size of a nat.

I took a taxi back to my apartment, passing the museum where government officials had groups of men laid on the ground in restraints. The taxi driver retold the story of a wild man, who without provocation, destroyed the treasures at the museum, which caused the authorities to arrive and wrestle everyone inside to the ground. Esteban's plan didn't produce the desired result of the locals revolting once they found out that the people's treasures were worthless replicas.

I sat in the taxi, taking in the sight of the Saratoga Hotel and the many government buildings that line Paseo del Prado. The beautiful complexions of my people that obediently stood the lines to food supply stores stretched around corners. It was sad to know that they were comfortable with their tarjetas where they were permitted to purchase basic rations of beans and rice. They were complacent. There was a wider world outside of Cuba, but they were a part of the thankful poor, and they didn't know it.

I instructed the driver to drop me off several blocks from the apartment. To his surprise, I handed him a stack of Cuban Pesos and told him to forget that he had ever saw me and for his safety to not report that he had been given the pesos. He understood the rules of the streets, where one should never get between a man and his ability to earn a living. However, I got the money was of no concern to him. It was his now.

Just as I turned onto the street to the apartment, I noticed several government cars parked in front of the building. Two sentinels stood at the entrance. They were surprised to see me as I walked to them and submitted my wrist to be restrained. Just as the last rung on the handcuffs clicked to a lock, Margara emerged from the building, escorted by two government men in suits. Tears filled her face as we locked stares. I had managed to maintain my composure until I heard her say, "Nosotros perdimos al bebe."

*****

I am writing this letter from an unknown confined cell. The guard that is tasked with my care has agreed to transmit my simple verses to any one of the human watch groups that has expressed concern with the conditions of political prisoners in Cuba. My decision to steal the currency was justified in that I consider it reparations for the land that was stolen from mi mama's family, the Batistas. For that act, the government can easily assign me as a common thief, an enemy of the state. No matter the classification, I state without reservation, that Yo soy un Cubano. Patria o Muerte is in my spirit, and as a patriot, I wish to be free from the oppressive regime that has plagued this land for over 50 years.

My wife, Margara Cepedes-Marti, if she has not been imprisoned, I am certain that every Sunday, she will walk the streets as a Damas de Blanco, holding a picture of me that bears my name and my service to Cuba.

Patri O Muerte Venceremos!

Jose Enrique Batista-Marti

FIN

CLIENT #5

There I was, awake, lying face up, studying the ceiling, a full five minutes before the three calls of pan – pan would herald in the new day. I had given up on the usual negotiations where I'd convince myself that I had earned the luxury to sleep for another five minutes.

I had reached my 40th year on Earth. The grey stubble has transitioned from the spotty salt and pepper phase that marked my 30's to an indelible pattern that would betray any lie that I could manufacture as it concerns my middle-aged status.

The spike of the androgenic hormone testosterone at 29 turned my once thick mane into a joke, where the scalp hair is only covering on the sides and the back of the head. Thankfully, I get to keep the knowledge of any by rising and performing the prescribed act where I separate my head in four quarters, and with the grace of a deli butcher, I traverse my head with a multi-blade razor until I achieve the look of a guy that chooses the sporty bald head, as opposed to a guy who is cursed with the affliction.

On my 40th, I couldn't get past what was painfully counting down to me for the last six months of sharing air with this girl who was three months shy of being half my age. I know my time with Olivia was temporary. She hasn't told me of the expiration date to this affair, nor has she indicated that she was leaning towards an exit, but the reality of being double her age plus 90 days was the only notice that was needed -- that our affair was furnished on condition that she held tight to the illusion that I was her "soul mate".

Olivia never had a full night of sleep; a byproduct of nights that blended into days as she chased every song to the last beat, no matter how dank of a hole it led her. Those years were behind me, and I couldn't pretend to be a night crawler in the way that Olivia was. Some nights, I wondered if she looked at the insides of her lids because by the time, I was fighting off the night's slumber, she stood fully awake, sipping a variation of hot water over crushed beans.

Lately, I've grown annoyed at what I was suspecting to be an intentional slight by Olivia, as a way to jumpstart a morning argument or maybe it was just a trait that was a reflection of her age group. Over the week, I'd stumble into the kitchen to shelve the honey and spices that she left scattered and clean up the milk that she spilt, when her selfishness of never replacing milk stared me in the face. I just recently done away with the notion that she would catch on to my desire for sweetener of some kind, so that I could soften my morning coffee – as suspected, self-centered behavior was all the rage with millennials.

On this morning, just as my anger reached its limit, Olivia buried herself into my arms while letting out a high pitched "Happy Birthday Georgie!" Her exuberant attitude half-heartedly convinced me that the affection was genuine, and more than ever on this day it served to disarm any contempt that had formed because I had to endure the punch that a sip of black coffee left on my tongue.

Olivia broke free of the embrace and retreated to my well-worn messenger bag that she appropriated months back and retrieved an oblong dark wood colored bottle of Kiehl's musk fragrance. Olivia was excited to share her knowledge about the fragrance and how it had "…originally created-in-the-like-200 years ago…" She continued with her less than accurate knowledge of a fragrance she should have full knowledge of as a saleswoman at Kiehl's. Putting aside Olivia's seductive tank top where her nipples protruded through, and the fleshy-follicle free mound that was framed behind whatever pastel colored panties she donned, I managed to key in on the insult that Olivia stole my gift – and I knew she stole it – and the laziness of her in not taking the box that it came in, nor removing the "TESTER" sticker that was affixed to the bottom of the bottle.

I had the evidence. I knew that the expiration date of the relationship had arrived, it was in front of me, and now in my hand, and because the musk agreed with my body's chemistry, I would have the evidence with me at least until the bottle was empty.

I thanked Olivia and watched as she beamed with pride, like a cat that had just laid a dead bird at your feet. Then a switch flipped in her mind as she made her way around me and into the kitchen where she removed all the honey and spices, I had just shelved and stopped when she noticed the empty carton of milk.

Another switch flipped off and on again. In that instance, Olivia blurted out that she'd just go to Starbucks to get a chai tea. I would've rested knowing Olivia was, at minimum, intellectually honest had she chosen the corner bodega over the corporate coffee chain that she railed against, whenever corporations were the bad guys on her social media feed.

The ruse of a happy relationship was over. What I had been avoiding for months was clearer on this day than it was six months prior: there was no future for me with Olivia. Viewing her world through her inner thigh gap or her gravity defying b-cups could only take a relationship so far. Her sexual appetite was healthy and that pleased me greatly, but even the newfound freedom that I was experiencing with Olivia was not enough to sustain a relationship.

I had a mortgage on a home that I didn't live in and child support payments that were older than the time Olivia had been of legal age. My rebirth with this young woman had ended. The problem for me now may be that I had never mastered the right way to end a relationship. I reasoned with the age difference I could fall on my sword, and maybe preserve a loose right of return by telling Olivia I believed that she should pursue someone in her age group; someone without child support who could keep up with her club/yoga regime.

While I was preparing a self-deprecating break-up speech, I failed to catch the look on Olivia's face as she made her exit.

After scanning the room, I noticed a note on the door that read: "I can NOT DO this. Your a good guy." The English teacher in me took over any bruising that my ego might've sustained as I realized Olivia didn't understand the difference between the possessive "your" and the contraction "you're", meaning you are.

Olivia's exit relieved me of the burden of having to care for her emotions. Her exit also denied me the possibility of future drunk one-last-time encounters. There I stood on my 40th, sipping a lukewarm cup of chalky coffee. There was no milk in the refrigerator, and my messenger bag was missing. I had a bottle of musk as a reminder of Olivia's love (or lack thereof) for me, and without fail, pan-pan rang out.

The alarm sound caused me to awake to the reality that I was free. Well, I still had the obligations of child support and a mortgage on the home my ex-wife lived in with our son. After paying rent on my one-room apartment, health insurances, setting aside metro and Uber payments I was left with $900 for entertainment or to add to my emergency fund.

My two oldest hobbies of playing poker and enjoying intimacy with a woman in a commercial transaction had been exercised out of my life since meeting Olivia. She never understood poker because of the time and financial commitments that the game demands, so to her, it was dismissed as "lame" and "shady". Early on, I dropped the argument because the money I saved on buy-ins went to bar tabs and yoga lessons. Transferring one activity for another would've been a positive, but where I had the potential of adding to my bank account with a game of poker, the most I could get out of yoga was in gaining a view of the sweaty end of the MILF brigade.

The rations that would usually be used in my weekly pilgrimage to Orchids of Asia was negligible at best because I was now providing sustenance for Olivia, and even with her on and off vegan-veggie diet, I was hit with sticker shock as she filled her hemp shopping bags with goji berries, buckwheat, organic-gluten free pasta or whatever else was on Gwyneth Paltrow's weekly Goop recommendation.

I knew that it was too early to get in a private game in the valley and the Uber fee to get to Hollywood Park Casino would cost the buy-in for a $40-$100 game, so the best thing I could do to celebrate my birth after conjuring up the image of Olivia's naked body floating through the apartment was to hope that I had enough funds to enjoy the day.

Olivia questioned me for showing interest in the *LA Times* story where Orchids of Asia raid was on the front page with the headline: Sex Shop Client List in City Attorney's Hand. I had never received a summons for court, so I reasoned that I was in the clear, but knew Orchids was not an option and the humiliation that comes with going through the reference checks when naked on a massage table when you're the new client always made my bowels irritable.

Begrudgingly, I called the one madam I knew, Hilda, who provided ex playmates, mattress actresses and thespians who had surpassed the age of being sought after or who just didn't have the talent that their local theatre group thought they had, and they realized that they could trade on their charm and maybe the *Pretty Woman* experience could be had.

Hilda ran a tight operation, and I knew that if I tried to haggle with her, she would blacklist me. I once joked with her about her no haggle pricing by repeating the Car Max slogan: "WBYCEIYDBO". She was dumbfounded at the word and thought that I was speaking in tongues. For nearly an hour I explained who Car Max is and why "WBYCEIYDBO" stood for, "We'll Buy Your Car Even If You Don't Buy Ours". Once understanding was established, Hilda readied her hand to smack at me, but instead advised me, "The girl I have for you will cost $400 for the hour. There will be no deals and don't do this American thing of talking about cars to explain your sexual appetite".

There wouldn't be any deals. The $200 that I budgeted for a massage parlor wouldn't get me far with Hilda. I checked my online balance, scanning the cleared purchases. I ran the list in my head of purchases that may be pending and eventually I accepted that I had $639 I could play with. I expected a direct deposit that was set to be posted to the account any day, the editing work I picked up with the publishing house would be a bump to my bank balance and my ego. I had tutoring jobs lined up and those payments didn't have a paper trail, so it was mine -- free and clear from the tax man and the ex-wife.

For safety, I checked the balance once again and reasoned that I could ask Hilda for a girl that would allow me a $400 experience. If the encounter was anything like the last girl, then a $100 tip would be in order. The goal would be to not fall in love – that's how I ended up with Olivia.

I disguised Hilda's number in my phone as Principal Hilda Gelavishi in case Olivia demanded access during one of her caffeine withdrawal episodes or if her insecurities set in when seeing me in conversation with any woman that she could gage to be past the age of 30, or any woman that may have known who Theroux, Nabokov or Hemmingway is.

There it was, Principal Hilda Gelavishi, with two asterisk symbols after the last name as a reminder that she wasn't an actual principal. It was my version of coded talk.

Her thick Georgian accent greeted me on the first ring. I didn't allow for a second of dead air from her "hello" and me establishing that an old client was back to patronize her services.

Me: Hilda, this is George.

Hilda: I know, I have caller identification.

Me: It is my birthday…

Hilda: There are no deals for birthdays.

Me: I understand. I have $400 as walk around money.

Hilda: You won't be walking far. I have an address for you. It is coming in text. Fall in love and you are what President Bush tried to explain.

Me: I know. Fool me once…Fool me…

Hilda: You can't get fooled again. Have fun. Just fun, not love.

Before the call ended, the address, number and name Simone came through text. I fired off a text to Simone: This is George. Referred by Hilda.

While awaiting a reply, I ran to the shower and examined who I had become under Olivia. Early on in the relationship, she convinced me that a shaved pubic area was better for hygiene and aesthetics. I was sold when she followed up with the suggestion that a bald area would make her want to be attached to it.

The relationship had reached its conclusion and the evidence rested in my examination. Not having shaved my pubes had me back on track to being restored to resembling my former caveman self. The boyish look had left in the week it took to grow.

I scanned the bathroom; Olivia's makeup bags were gone. Stumbling out of the bathroom, I pulled open the drawers and saw that she had emptied them. It was clear that her exit was premeditated. How long had she known?

My inquiries were interrupted by the buzzing sound of an incoming message. On shaky, wet feet, I hurried to the phone on the tips of my toes, punch in my code and read the message from Simone: "Client #5, I will be available for the next 2 hours. Upscale Hollywood Condominium is where I take in-calls. Can you confirm?"

Not knowing if I was the fifth client of the day or if the title of Client #5 was her way of cultivating the illusion that she was a sought-after professional who arraigned her clients in numerical order. I paused before responding and typed the response: "Yes, I look...", and paused, thinking that a long message could appear too eager, so, I erased and typed a simple response, less enthusiastic: YES.

Opening the Uber app, I saw that there were 8 cars in the area. The drive from Brentwood to Simone's upscale Hollywood condominium should take me 39 minutes and cost $24 dollars but would be lowered to $20 for a shared ride. Having been redirected mere blocks from my destination in the past, I opted for the $24 dollar ride in Habib's Prius.

My city has changed over the years. The landmarks have added new characters. New condominium structures have replaced the Tiffany Theatre on Sunset and boutique hotels now sprinkled The Strip. It seems like rock 'n roll died when Kurt Cobain died, and that was a long time ago. On the drive east, new, and repurposed loft buildings gave way to the studios that make up the Sunset/Gower corridor. Habib wasn't much into small talk, which allowed me to play out my repertoire when with a working girl. I'd keep it simple – no kissing, no cunnilingus – I'd direct her start on top, then move into power position once she was well oiled.

Driving further east on Hollywood Blvd, the new developments had ended, and I began a silent prayer, hoping that the "upscale condominium" that Simone had advertised was tucked behind the dank building that Habib had deposited me in front of - 5205 Hollywood Blvd didn't have a luxury street sign, let alone a luxury entrance. There was the rundown El Adobe liquor store and the Dog Resort on the ground level and upon further inspection of the grounds, I could make out that the living quarters of this mixed-use building sat behind a black grilled gate.

I texted Simone, and within seconds, a waif drifted down the stairs. I couldn't place her accent or appearance to any region. She wore ill-fitting skinny jeans that were baggy in the back pockets. Her black hoodie sweatshirt was faded from one-to-many washes and the lettering that spelled the brand name Supreme down the arms looked to be stained with mustard on the "S" in the word.

To my surprise, she greeted me with a kiss on the lips. Before the fear of a cold sore transmission could form in my mind, Simone interlocked our hands and pulled at me to follow her up the stairs. The smell of stripper grade Victoria Secret perfume trailed her as we passed neighboring apartments where stacks of succulent plants lined the common area. I read the note on apartment #3 that said, "Deliveries can be left with Simone, the manager in #5". So, she was the manager of the building and an escort. At least the thought of being rolled by a pimp had ended. If she managed the building, then she wouldn't be mobile as if she could uproot and set up shop in another location.

Simone flung open the door to #5 and the smell of cat urine overpowered the heavy perfume she had dosed herself with. I keyed in on two bird cages full of a family of cockatoos who served as an alarm system as they wailed bloody murder upon seeing me. Simone shushed at them while covering my eyes as she continued to lead me to her bedroom where she entertained clients.

She said, "Gorgeous George, nice to meet you." Even though I hadn't had much time to process the room, I was able to see past Simone's tiny frame and notice the pile of clothes that had collected in the corner. My attention shifted to the Backstreet Boys posters that lined the walls. If I hadn't studied the smile lines that were present at the corners of her mouth and on her forehead, I would've bolted for the door, thinking I was with an adolescent.

Before I could respond to Simone attempts at being cute by cocking her hip to the side like she was preparing to break out into a pep cheer, or the name "Gorgeous George" that she kept repeating, she backed out of the room with her finger to her mouth for me to "shush", then she whispered, "Place the donation on the counter."

The dark sheets that draped the window didn't allow for much light to expose all the flaws in the room. The bed sheets appeared clean and I was already committed, so in my attempt at anticipating danger and having counted out the "donations" ahead of time, I undressed in a systematic order, not forgetting the tricks I learned over the years: bury my wallet and watch into my shoe; then pack the shoe with my socks; and place my shirt on top of the shoes and fold my pants and place it on top of the shirt. If I needed a quick exit, the plan would be to reverse the process with my pants going on first, then my shirt and if time permitted, I'd retrieve my wallet and watch or run for the door with my shoes in hand.

Simone entered with music emanating from her mobile phone. I gave her credit for her choice of Annie Lennox's "Walking on Broken Glass". I subtracted favorable points as I took in Simone's cotton panty/tank top choice that confirmed that she was tone deaf to the experience that a proper call-girl can provide by investing in a lacy frock or even a house coat.

Simone motioned for me to lay back. This was the first time that I was able to acknowledge a face that had once been cute, pretty even, but had long ago succumbed to being weathered, which no amount of makeup could disguise.

I was naked and propped up against the headboard while Simone stared at me with a lazy gaze from the end of the bed. In a whisper, she struggled with the Spanish pronunciation of, "close your eyes", "Cierra Tus Ojos". A request I was not going to participate in, so I lowered my gaze while keeping my sight on her as she kneeled like she was retrieving something from under the bed, which prompted me to prepare for a fight.

Before I could brace myself to exit the bed Simone emerged with a puppet in each hand and launched into dialogue between the puppets that were modeled after Hillary Clinton and Donald Trump. I couldn't run, and her puppets had now piqued my curiosity in what this play would evolve into. "Good thing you're not the president," she motioned, as if the Hillary puppet was lurching forward, while she held the Trump puppet motionless, lowering her voice to imitate Trump's matter of fact deliver, "Because you'd be in jail."

It clicked that I was watching Simone put on the 2016 presidential debate highlights with puppets. It was painfully clear that it could only go to a darker place from here and without protest from Simone, who by now was alternating her voice impersonations from Hillary to Trump with ease, I retrieved my clothes without any immediacy and reversed the process that I had practiced: placing my pants on first, then my shirt and pulled up my socks, deposited my wallet into my pocket and latched my watch right as the music switched to MC Hammer's "Pumps and a bump…we like the girls with the pumps and a bump…". Simone abandoned the political puppets and launched into a spasm routine, completely oblivious that I had stood and retrieved my "donation" from the side table as I exited the room.

Standing at the front door, the cockatoo's released a mocking laugh. The cat walked towards me and stopped, as if he was a bouncer directing me out of a dive bar. Maybe the joke was on me. If it was, I carried out the only protest that I could muster by hurrying to the cockatoo's cage where I flipped the latch, hoping that they would fly out of the door that I left open as I bolted out of there.

FI

TICK-TOCKERS

Every day, Joe arrives home from work at 6:10 p.m. As it usually does in late March, the evening daylight lasted longer. With his clock-based schedule, he never adjusted his daily activities. His fastidious approach to life had served him well as he rose from the position of parking enforcer for the City of Beverly Hills to regional civil enforcement officer in the traffic control division in under four years – a distinction he was sure to advise parking inspectors that were charged with training new officers. Joe constantly reminded the inspectors that he was responsible for getting ordinances passed that made it a civil infraction, punishable by a $10 fine for citizens to lash out at parking enforcement officers and calling them "meter maids" while they were carrying out their official duty as the timekeepers of order on city curbs and parking structures.

It usually took a year before enforcement officers under Joe's command excused his verbose morning briefings or his incessant radio updates, on everything from traffic flow to locations of potential violators of "order", as he referred to anyone whose quarter panel extended into the red by two centimeters or anyone who mismanaged their schedule by allowing the countdown clock to reach zero.

Joe reveled in blocking his schedule in units of time. To eliminate boredom and to mimic meter violations, he set countdowns to indicate the time remaining before his next attack. At home, Joe arranged the screensavers on his computer and the television to act as the countdown sequence at the start of old films, restarting at 10 once it reaches 1.

From the moment he entered the door at 6:10 p.m., he engaged the straight baton hands with a tap of the chronograph pusher on his Omega Speed Master, permitting himself 60 seconds to remove one bean and cheese burrito form the freezer and placing it in the microwave for a 3-minute nuking.

Once the burrito was in, Joe would remove the pitcher of water from the refrigerator and retrieve a glass from the cupboard, pouring a cup 4 centimeters high and consuming the water before placing the cup in the sink and returning the pitcher, then spinning on his heels to the sink where he rinsed the cup, before placing it in the drying rack, then consulting the seconds hand wherein he confirmed that he had 5 seconds left on the 60-second nuke job.

Joe grinned as he watched the countdown on the microwave reflect 2:03, 2:02, 2:01 seconds where he adjusted the bezel to allow the minute hand 120 ticks to meet his mark. At the 2:00 mark on the microwave, Joe was returned to the moment by a bark. He pivoted a full 180 degrees, allowing his smile to increase as he took in the image of a barrel-chested bulldog whose wagging nub of a tail indicated playfulness. "Good evening, Benny," Joe said, as he grabbed the leash on the counter as Benny stepped forward and presented his neck for shackling.

The two exited the door at the same speed, with Joe estimating Benny's distance to be 18 centimeters ahead of him as he maintained a taught tether, not allowing much opportunity for free reign.

Joe engaged the pusher at the 3-meter mark of the walk and without issuing an order, Benny stepped onto the grass, hunching his back in preparation of business matters. Just as Joe turned his back, affording Benny privacy, he noticed a blonde wearing a tight-fitting white shirt, less than 6 meters away. The buoyancy to her chest caused the shirt to expose her midsection and as she closed the distance from the tree where her snow-white bulldog had finished business, she half-heartedly struggled to keep control of the animal charging at Benny.

Benny kicked his hind legs to cover his waste and stepped to Joe's side, wagging his tail as the blond and the snow-white dog approached. "Hi, I'm Laura and this is Maggie," she said. Joe consulted his watch, where he acknowledged that 30 seconds remained on his schedule.

"I'm Joe and this is Benny," he said. Laura released light laughter as Maggie and Benny exchanged sniffs to kick off their inspection of one another.

"Like Benny Hill? Oh my, and you're British, I hear your accent," she said.

Joe flipped his wrist to view the time, noticing that 26 seconds remained. "Yes, I'm British, from Bromley."

"I'm from Venice..., California. How long have you been living in Marina Del Rey?" Laura asked, while working Maggie's leash from becoming entangled with Benny's.

Joe considered providing the exact year, day and hourly breakdown, but instead responded, "Oh, a little shy of 4 years."

Laura released Maggie's leash, abandoning the effort of maintaining order. She raised her shoulders in a sign of defeat, causing her breast to bounce long after her gesture ended.

Joe looked down at Benny who was fully engaged in an affair with Maggie as he realized that he would fail to maintain his schedule if he didn't return to his door. Raising his head, he reviewed his watch then continued looking up where he took in the bifurcated framing in Laura's cut off jean shorts. His eyes traveled higher and rested on the recognizable tongue and lip logo of the Rolling Stones on Laura's shirt. Their eyes met. A bead of sweat formed on Joe's upper lip as his countdown reached zero. Knowing that his regimented life had ended, he released a nervous smile that also served as an apology for his elevator eyes and as a truce, Laura grinned while asking, "So, are you a Stones or Beatles fan?"

***

The fear that came with Laura asking a stranger question that she would ordinarily refuse to answer herself took a backseat to her surprise that she had stepped out of the house in cut-off shorts and a body-hugging T-shirt; the exact type of outfit that she detested all through college as she felt that displaying oneself in suggestive clothes was a desperate attempt at gaining attention. Her read of Joe's nervousness only helped forward the idea that she was thrusting her sexuality onto him as she was unaware that his primary concern rested in his now messy schedule, and the bean and cheese burrito that would harden if he reheated it upon returning.

Laura debated whether she should make a formal apology, but instead, settled on the inquiry into his preference for The Rolling Stones or The Beatles. The relief that came with Joe's smile and the boyish way that he pointed at The Rolling Stones tongue and lip logo allowed Laura's fear to subside.

Just 120 seconds prior, she stood on the inside of her door, whipping sweat from her forehead as she repeated the words, "Time don't own me. I use it // it doesn't use me." Two sentences that she employed as a mantra that helped her when she turned her locks based on the numbers that appeared on the second hand of her watch. One hundred seconds before the reciting of the mantra, she stood at the dining table, studying the line-up of watches she arranged from left to right, in order from oldest to latest acquisition. Stopwatches that marked decades of technology and the complexities of artisans of time keeping, like Audemars Piguet, Blacpain, to precision second splitters that range from TAG Huer, Seiko, followed by the plastic quartz track watches of Swatch and Nike.

The timepieces were useful instruments in Laura's life, which allowed her to keep a schedule, or as she often repeated, "To keep the trains on time." The lengths she went to in concealing her watches and to engage pushers while in her pockets were accomplished with motor skills that had been perfected over the years. Had anyone known the prestidigitation that was being employed throughout the day, she would've received ovations for the entertainment value, but the manipulation was her secret that she believed she had become a servant of.

Laura kept her right hand in her pocket where she ran her thumb over the pusher to her trusted Huer pocket watch, ready to stop or start a task and memorialize the event in her leger – an act that she had come to realize had gotten away from her as she had filled a storage unit with boxes of legers that marked her life since arriving at university four years prior.

Laura committed this day as her first day where she would not possess a watch and abandon the need to listen to the ticking as a task began or relish the feel of engaging a button twice: once to stop the sweeping hand as a task ended and the second click which returned that hand to the top of the hour.

Laura had completed a dual-MBA/Law program at Pepperdine University in two years. She was recruited at a civil litigation firm in large part because of the speed and detail that she completed brief writing. After two years at the firm, she overheard colleagues discussing her quirky behavior of keeping her hand in her pocket and the mechanical way that she spoke in burst, rarely taking a breath while citing case law. One colleague remarked that her behavior was the reason she was never assigned a case to present before a judge. She knew the colleague's gossip was true as she reflected on her task being limited to writing briefs and the occasional excursion to a courthouse simply to serve as a functionary who only interacted with court clerks.

Today was the day that she saw it necessary to abandon her use of stop watches to mark her life's moment. The muscle memory that had been built would be impossible to abandon completely, so even without a watch to mark transitions, counting and applying split second breakdowns would remain. Freeing her hand and reducing her speech to a speed that indicated she was in fact breathing, should, over time, instill confidence in the partners she was capable of administering justice on an oral level.

Laura abandoned her usual cargo pants and hooded sweatshirt uniform style that was a holdover from her college experience. She believed a bolder clothing arraignment would serve as a visual cue that she was out of her comfort zone and embracing the uncertainty that comes with living without a minute-by-second regimen.

The training she employed in her life had extended to Maggie, who up until now, had shared Laura's precision-tuned life – rise at 6:00 a.m.; exit the door 2 minutes later for her morning release; return 2 minutes later for the morning meal; exit 6:10 a.m. for another release; and at 6:45 a.m., say good day to Laura whom she wouldn't see until 6:10 p.m. when the schedule would resume.

Nudging Maggie to run free towards George and Benny wasn't a part of the plan; for Laura it was a perfect way to relieve herself of the usual walking path in the opposite direction and a rebuke of her normal timetable - although, she continued to count the steps as she closed the distance to George.

***

"So, The Stones…I agree." Laura said to Joe, who by now had begun to eye his door, not knowing how to excuse himself. "That's an Omega Speed Master," Laura said.

"Yes, it was a gift from my father," Joe replied, as he stood astounded at Laura's excitement as she eyed the 60-second revolution of the hand.

"I better not. It is a beauty. The link between the past and the future," Laura said while continuing her examination. Pointing at the watch, Laura said to Joe, "Engage the pusher and let the time run. I'll give you 120 seconds to tell me about yourself and then I'll take the same to tell you about me."

Joe considered the proposition as he focused on his door that was 3 meters behind Laura, then refocusing his sight as he settled on Laura's face. He pushed the button that engaged the hand for the small seconds sub dialer and noticed that Laura's smile had increased.

Joe met her smile with a devilish grin as he said, "My mother said to start a story with a fact or in a way a child would recognize it to be a bedtime story." Shaking her head as a sign that she agrees, Laura said, "Once upon a time it is."

FIN

EMOTIONS

    Victor Maitland, "the Queen of all Queens" as everyone in the office lovingly called him, was having his annual Halloween party and everyone in the accounting department he ran was invited. Charles hadn't been in the department long, but since receiving the invitation a week ago, he worried that he wouldn't be able to find a costume that fit the specifications that Victor spelled out in his video invite: "You must come dressed as a human emotion. Be creative and prove to everyone that you aren't just a bean counter. We like numbers, especially anything above 6 inches. I'm just joshing – not really."

    Charles had watched the video no less than 20 times, and with every viewing, he broke out in a sweat, not knowing what he could wear that could fit his 6'5" frame. There aren't too many options at costume stores when you weigh 250 pounds. "A human emotion," Charles said to himself after watching the video for the last time on the night of the party, unsure if he would make a good impression or if he would never get an invitation to one of Victor's legendary parties.

    Charles stood at his refrigerator, opened the door, and retrieved a Bartlett pear that matched the size of his massive fist he had balled up. Placing the pear next his jet-black skin, the sweat beads began to form, causing Charles to abandon the thought.

***

    Joanie, the tiny brunette who ran the office like a mouse, stood at Penthouse #2 where from inside the apartment, she could hear the faint sound of Madonna's song "Like a prayer." Just as she reached for the doorbell, Victor, dressed in a white suit with huge angle wings, flung open the door and saw Joanie dressed in a fire engine red latex one piece suit, replete with plastic horns and a three-prong pitchfork in one hand.

Victor and the crowd that assembled behind him, who were all dressed in some variation of white suits and body-hugging leather outfits, masked their interest in Joanie's decision to wear red, which caused Joanie to cringe, thinking that she had missed the idea of the dress code.

"What are you supposed to be?" Victor asked, with his distinctive lisp overpowering his surfer boy persona.

"I'm passion. Fire," Joanie said, with hesitation, awaiting Victor's approval.

Victor looked back at the crowd, issued an eye wink, and then turned back to Joanie and immediately took her into his arms saying, "Yes girl. You are fierce! I knew she was hiding a killer body under all those frumpy clothes that she wears. Get in here."

Joanie beams with pride as she enters the apartment to cheers and hugs.

Five minutes later.

Peter O'Malley, the professional alcoholic of the office who brags he never gets drunk, reaches for the doorbell, and stops as Victor flings open the door. "Peter! Green?" Victor asks, as his eyes Peter's green suit from top to bottom like a retina scan machine.

"I'm green. Greed. Envy," Peter says with a devilish grin as he watches Victor's smile form.

"You sexy motherfucker. Somebody, get this Mick a Heineken," Victor says while ushering Peter into the apartment.

Thirty minutes later.

Followed by the crowd dressed in white with Peter in green and Joanie in her red suit, Victor opens the door to a naked Charles who has a pear stuck to his erect penis. Victor, nor the crowd is able to hide their shock, confusion and pleasure at Charles naked body.

Seconds past and Victor summons the courage to ask, "What is going on Charles, are you alright?"

Confused by the question, Charles responds, "Man, I'm fucking-dis-pear!"

Victor and the crowd erupt in laughter as Victor wraps his arm around Charles, eyeing the pear as he leads him into the apartment, adding, "Charles, you are going places in life young man."

FIN

THE PITCH

"Let me tell you about the rich." David said, before reaching for his cup of espresso. I had never known him to play it up for an audience, especially during our time at Beverly Hills High, he never played into the "types" that had been laid out. Without exaggeration, everyone at Beverly was rich -- some families flaunted their wealth, like the Persian kids who all drove BMW's and E-class Mercedes as soon as they received their learners permits. This was the early 90s and wearing the latest Guess, Armani, or one of the silk Versace shirts with the head of Medusa emblazoned on the front and back put fashionistas on notice that Milanese playboy ambitions that were carefully cultivated over the summer holiday were being exercised in the halls of Beverly.

Where the Persian kids led in the sports car arena, they were also front runners in the cosmetic surgery field. Rhinoplasty over summer or winter break served as cover for a girl to reintroduce herself to her classmates that had known her since preschool.

In 1994, Sarah Shimon, whose father was rumored to be an Israeli arms dealer, set a new trend when she came back from break with a noticeably fuller chest. Sarah stood 5'9", with a proper hip-to-shoulder ratio that could easily sustain 36 Cs. But all through junior high, when rosebuds blossomed into full B's and C-Cups, Sarah flat-lined to an unimpressive A.

Emerging from out of her father's security chauffeured S-Class, the gaggle of Libby's, Beth's, Tara's and Olivia's cleared a path as Sarah covered the distance from the curb to the entrance like a catwalk had been laid before her.

Unlike the rich kids whose family adorned them with the trappings of wealth just because they attended school, David's self-imposed dress code was a variation of chinos and a polo shirt and a carefully folded sweater and blazer in his bag. Occasionally, I'd overhear the grunge clique chattering in sotto voce as David made his way through the halls, "The future president...commander-in-chief", which was all meant to poke fun at David's style. They were wanna-be Kurt Cobains, wherein David looked like he was in a perpetual auditioning state for membership into the Flat Hat Club.

Everyone knew that David's father was the head of Paramount Pictures and he had produced hits like *American Gigolo, Raiders of the Lost Ark, Reds, Flash Dance*, and was the architect that made Eddie Murphy and Tom Cruise box office bankable, while collecting Oscars for *Ordinary People* and *Terms of Endearment* on his rise to gracing *Time,* as the Most Influential Man in Hollywood. *Forbes* topped *Time* the following year by bestowing the title of "The Most Powerful Man in Hollywood", yet David never traded on his father's name, nor did he ever take advantage of the ingénue, or their mothers who tried to ingratiate themselves to him, hoping to gain access with David Sr. David was tone-deaf to the groupies that cheered for him at Beverly's lacrosse games; he had monastic focus on the task of penetrating the crease.

"Beverly was a blur. Nouveau riche without direction or bumpers to keep you in your lane is a recipe for disaster. How many times did you want to pop one of those kids?" David's question allowed me to segue into a tale that continues to reverberate through the halls of Beverly and UCLA. In our senior year, it was rumored that David was at a UCLA football team party and was challenged by a quartet of anabolic steroid abusers - when the dust cleared, there was a stack of UCLA players snoring a musical composition and David had vanished.

I had to ask him, "Was the UCLA brawl real or legend?" David allowed a smile to form while he retrieved two cigars from a leather case. He clipped the business end and handed one to me, and before I could protest, a concentrated stream of fire was cremating the compressed tobacco. David lit his cigar without succumbing to a coughing episode like the one I had. I didn't know if smoking was permitted at this café, and not wanting to come off as uncultured to the prerogatives that cigar smokers enjoyed, I reasoned it best to follow his lead with the inhale-release routine, all while waiting for him to confirm the legendary story.

"You heard the story from Beckwith?" Without a second of dead air, I responded, "Yes." Then David's response came: "Beckwith and Francine were dating and the night you speak of, *Pulp Fiction* was playing at the Fox Theatre. If you can recall, they recited Travolta and Samuel's lines for the remainder of the school year." David pulled on his cigar and released a plume of smoke into the sky, allowing me time to run through the calendar where the impromptu recitals by Beckwith and Francine took form in my mind-eye. In the halls or in the middle of history class, they would find it necessary to launch into renditions of Vincent and Jules hyper violent, profanity laced dialogue, replete with every "fuck" that highlighted the start or end to a sentence.

"If Beckwith was at the Fox Theatre for the 8 p.m. show, it would be impossible for him to be at the party by 8:30 p.m. when these jocks were napping on the grass."

I wasn't sure if eliminating Beckwith as an eyewitness meant that the incident didn't happen. It was clear that David didn't offer a denial that the incident involved him, so, for clarity, I decided to be direct, "Did you KO the guys?" With a devilish grin, David leaned forward, modulating his speaking voice to a whisper, and said, "Absolutely, 100% not guilty." The denial induced a laugh out of me. "So, modeling a denial after OJ Simpson plea is odd company." Without rushing, David said, "What was the verdict?" I retorted, "Not guilty…doesn't mean he didn't do it." I thought that by adding the caveat would shake his decision to employ and OJ'ism - considering that the "not guilty" verdict wash couched in less than certainty - but instead, he did what I had seen him do from grade school throughout our time at Beverly - he reminded me, "[that] you are too warrior-minded. Put down your sword and the battle will go away."

David provided calm. I hadn't seen him in 10 years and here I was pestering him for answers on a story that was 25 years in the past. The time before that was in 2001. I had finished my masters at NYU and was fresh off an Academy nomination. On a press stop in Belgium, I happened upon David in a café. He was sitting with three men, all four wore yarmulkes and as David approached, I noticed the fringes of his tzitzits dangling at his sides. Without mention of the six-year gap since high school, we agreed that we would meet at my hotel for dinner to catch up.

David enjoyed the stories I shared about classmates that went off to Stanford, Princeton..., those who went into law, journalism, medicine..., who had gotten married. I didn't realize it at the time, but he directed all of my inquiries into his life back to a question about me and my work in documentary films, playing on my desire to share the corners and alleys my subjects took me to, and before I knew it, the night had ended and I was leaving Antwerp, not knowing what David had done in life, why he was in Antwerp, or on which continent he lived. When I congratulated him on his father's success in the *Mission Impossible* franchise, his reply was absent any contempt or excitement. It was neutral at best. He said, "I imagine it was a monumental undertaking".

It was an interesting observation to study David as he stood at the curb where he extinguished his cigar with a cup of water, then oddly, instead of flicking the cigar like cigarette smokers do once they finish, he placed the moist butt into a napkin.

His appearance had evolved from the chino-polo variation that marked his adolescent years and had given way to bespoke suits. Nothing ostentatious to direct the audience to imagine a career in banking, entertainment, or the legal profession. The time piece he wore was an austere Patek Phillipe with a leather band. There were no diamonds on the bezel, no pinky rings adorning either hand. His frame appeared firm, resolute, like he maintained the boxing discipline that always angered his father, who preferred that he focus on lacrosse or tennis.

As David took a sip of cappuccino, I made a statement at the risk of offending him, "Something happened to you David." He eyed me, and for a second, I was back in bar mitzvah class with him when he first instilled fear in me and most of the other boys after we witnessed him dispatching a grown adult who was harassing us on the streets. If the beating that he unleashed wasn't enough for the man's ego, David made the man apologize to the group.

I continued, "You've always been able to kick my ass. The heaviest item I've carried in the last 15 years has been my wife's luggage and it has wheels." David's trademark cocked headed laugh appeared and I was disarmed, yet still desiring answers. "David, you disappeared. No one knows where you went, if it was to college, what kind of work you do…" Before I could go any further, he showed me the palms of his hands while pushing against the air. "Yet, here I am, having a conversation." I wasn't going to let him off the hook. "It's true, you are, but I still don't know shit. I didn't connect with you on Facebook. You don't have social media. You are a ghost. You've been an enigma since freshman year at Beverly. I used to sleepover at your house every weekend, then in an instance, you became unavailable." "I became a man, with responsibilities. I had to work," he said, still not allowing a frown to create lines on his forehead.

In nearly 25 years, that was the most insight that David has given into his life. In 2001 when we had a moment in Antwerp, I never knew what he was doing there, and he never introduced me to the men he sat with. At his father's funeral 8 years later, he sat Shiva for the prescribed mourning period and all our graduating class hoped we would have a chance to catch up with him, to exchange information, get lunch if he was going to be in town, yet not knowing if he lived in town. Shiva provided him the perfect cover in not having to talk about anything but the life and death of his father, which he allowed his Uncle Fred and younger sister Rebecca to carry on with – a duty they revealed in.

David finished his cappuccino and I thought that he was going to excuse himself and that it would be the last time I saw him until he reappeared in another 10 years, then he said, "Paul, your life is exactly how you arranged it to be. You are on course. You followed your script. Your only fear may be that you hope that your best work is ahead of you and that you didn't top out with your first documentary. What you just did the one about the lady who abandoned her kid to study lions…" "Jane Hirsh. Yeah, we got snubbed - politics." I couldn't resist clarifying, "Yes, I saw it. You didn't say it explicitly, but any observer would say that she was manipulated, and she abandoned her child." David's words trailed off as I shook my head in the affirmative. David continued, "In the book by Palahniuk, he writes, 'We're the middle children of history…no purpose or place, we have no Great War, no Great Depression, our great war is a spiritual war, our depression is our lives.'" And then he paused as the waitress stepped toward our table.

"Is there anything else I can get for you gentlemen?" she asked. I didn't want to break my silence and it was the reason that David stopped with what I hoped to be information on who he had become in this spiritual war that he had discovered that I was unknowingly engaged in. "How about two waters with lime. You good with that?" I nodded and then watched with admiration as David delivered a line to the waitress, "la vie est belle." The waitress allowed her smile to reveal her gapped front teeth. With the charm of a schoolgirl, she briefly closed her eyes and replied, "tous les jours je suis reconnaisant." Her smile grew larger when David followed up with, "merci". I dared not interrupt what may have been David's attempt to entertain or his angle to recruit the waitress to be his confederate and carry out his plot to poison me for intruding into his life. I knew that my choice in learning Mandarin instead of French would haunt me, so at the mercy of David I awaited my water.

Once she disappeared, David turned his attention back to me and without any pride in his exchange, he said "Excuse me." With admiration for his approach and hoping that flattery would prompt him to continue I said, "I don't know what that was, but you lifted her spirits." The often-repeated smile-head tilt returned before he continued. "I had that understanding of where I was in life when going to Beverly." My puzzled expression allowed David to clarify. "That great war awaited me." I nodded, hoping to coax him to reveal more than the unknown Great War that he spoke of.

David tapped the table next to my phone and said, "Show me your Facebook." "Are you going to set up a profile?" I blurted out, while watching David as he eyed the waitress that had just returned with waters. "Merci," rolled out of her mouth in a sing song voice which prompted David to smile. "Yes, I'll set up a profile." "Excellent, you'll come tonight around 8 p.m." I figured if David agreed to set up a social media profile, he would reveal information about who he has between for the last 25 years, and if he showed up tonight, enough people would get turns at probing David's secretive world. "8 p.m. it is." That is all I said as I opened the Facebook app, turning the phone to David who viewed my profile, toggling with ease.

"Do you remember Sheena Klein?" I asked, while studying David for a clue that he was going to bolt. "Yes," David replied, with fondness in his eyes. "8 p.m., her house. What's your cell, I'll text you, her address?" I thought I would finally have a connection to David, but I realized that I hadn't seen him with a phone. I expected an excuse of some kind, but instead, he said, "What's her address?" while standing in preparation to leave. He handed me my phone, where I scrolled through my contacts and came to Sheena Klein name and rambled off the address in an irritated tone, like a jilted lover would when stonewalled for attention, "683 S. June St."

David removed a $100 bill from a modest stack of what I presumed were all Benjamins and left it on the table. "Off of Wilshire, Hancock Park." I was impressed with his mastery of the city, 'Like a fucking Thomas Guide." My reference to antiquated methods of navigation served as the levity needed for David to chuckle, then without prideful spiking of the ball, he recited the following: "1502 N. Croft, 7234 La Jolla, 8170 Melrose. 7-5-2-5..., 0-2-9. I'll see you tonight." Our hands met in a clench. I was without a comeback as I realized that David had remembered the addresses to my father's rental properties that we worked at in the summers, cutting grass for extra money and the reciting of my parent's home phone number 7-5-2-5-0-2-9, showed that his memory was sharper than mine. He didn't add the prefix, 213, because there was only 213 and 818 at the time, and if the caller originated from the same area code, only the seven-digit number was needed.

David turned and walked west on Melrose. He extended the distance from the café with the confident gait of an athlete. Out of courtesy and curiosity if he accepted my offer, I shouted, "I can give you a lift wherever you're going." The words trailed off in the wind, never reaching David's ears as my view of him was obscured by the legion of Japanese tourists that spilled out onto the sidewalk as they jockeyed for position to take selfies at Paul Smith pink wall.

I expected that I wouldn't see him again. He came as he wished and disappeared into space whenever he was finished doing whatever it was, he was up to. What was it that I was holding onto – the memory of a friend that I knew decades ago? The man who directed the simplest of inquiries back to the inquisitor and in an ingenious way, creating the environment that all the world's attention was directed at their life.

Immediately, I phoned friends who awaited my update on this lunch meeting. Sheena's adolescent crush had blossomed into middle aged lust that she reasoned could be explained away as a resurgence of irrational exuberance – the husband of 15 years and the two kids would be left to pick up the pieces once the affair that she had been cultivating in her dreams since high school vanished – in her estimation, this was a strong possibility for her.

He had maintained secrecy surrounding his life, and had he died, I doubt that anyone would've known. The last three encounters he managed to evade any revelation about his world. If he could get away with that tonight, considering the group that awaited him, I'd be left with the next plausible thought: that he had been incarcerated for drugs or a bank heist gone wrong, or was in the CIA or some secretive Mossad agent. Possibly a combination of the three. That's it – he was captured while on a CIA-Mossad mission and spent the years in between our encounters confined in some Iranian prison.

8:00 p.m. –

"Do you think he is married or maybe he…shit, I can't believe I'm nervous," Sheena said, as she wringed at her hands as if she was trying to remove her skin before she abandoned the thought and scurried off to set out the charcuterie board of cheeses, she took great care in preparing. Liz and Maria laughed with me, knowing that Sheena continued to hold onto the memory of the summer in '93 when David allowed her to accompany him to the movies. Of course, she interpreted the encounter to being an official date on a date.

"She better temper her exuberance or Thomas will be filling for divorce for real this time," Liz whispered with Maria cutting her off to say, "It's one thing that she allows herself to get caught up with cabana boys while drunk on girls' weekends in Cabo, but I doubt he will go for sharing emotional space with a ghost…that's what David is, a ghost." I found myself employing David's head tilt-laugh as I said, "Give her the moment. The fucker has charisma." I added, "If you had seen the way he had the waitress eating out of his hands, Liz, you'd dump Marvin, and Maria de la Paz-Cohen over here would slit my neck while I slept and run away with David." The two consulted their thoughts with devilish grins prompting Maria to add, "I wouldn't slit your throat but maybe I'd stage a break in."

Sheena entered the conversation, depositing grapes from one hand to her mouth with assembly line precision, only pausing as she noticed David standing near the door in conversation with her husband, Thomas, breaking her silence, but not her stare to say, "He fucking looks good. I think I'll talk with a divorce attorney tomorrow." Sheena walked to the crowd that had formed around David and stood at the outer rim, hoping that he noticed her.

Liz and Maria turned on their heels and joined the group. The 25 years since high school has borne witness to Maria becoming a tenured professor of Greek literature at UCLA; Liz has headed up three franchises for Disney, and if the chatter around town was true, the announcement that she would be named CEO was imminent; Marvin's hedge fund had a market cap of over $1,000,000,000. Our class produced several lawyers, doctors, dentists, film producers and a couple of federal prisoners, but as soon as David entered the room, all these accomplished adults reverted to insecure adolescents who had finally been allowed audience with the toughest, most charismatic enigma that made up our world.

I watched from a safe distance. David didn't appear overwhelmed by the attention; he had to expect that this would be the reaction. I caught his attention with a wave of my hand and then retreated to the charcuterie platter where I continued to watch as Sheena balanced her desire to be in David's embrace and honoring her vows to her husband who formed the group that consumed David's vision.

In a moment of pride for having been the one that has had the most interaction with David over the years, and having been the only non-family member to serve as pall bearer at his father's funeral, the mythical status David had achieved at Beverly and in the decades since had been transferred to me – even greater amounts than what had been bestowed upon Eden Farooq who bragged about having spent time with David in Botswana three years ago when she was on business with her third husband.

Viewing the frenzy from a distance allowed me the opportunity to see what the female species looks like when in heat and a dominant male enters the herd. The fawning and exaggerated hugs were evidence that women, innately responded to strength, mystery, and old-world discernment - traits that marked David's character throughout his time at Beverly. Maria and Liz constantly compared the sissified era of heartthrobs to men from bygone eras like Brando, Johnny Cash, Omar Sharif and without fail, David's name made the list of men that personified manliness. Liz would often say of the talent that have been cast in her films that, "They all seem to be waiting for some woman to comb their hair, to take them on a walk. None make you feel like they will chop a tree down, kill their dinner and then rearrange your mind in bed."

David managed to avoid playing the small talk game throughout the years at Beverly. He didn't belong to a clique, but after decades as a ghost, he was trapped in the mosh pit, only being saved or rather advancing to another layer of interrogation by Liz who dragged him to a group where Eden, Sheena, Brad and Michael awaited with their list to crosscheck.

I retreated to the backyard and unwrapped the Montecristo I bought. Actually, I purchased a box with the hopes that David would join me, and the others would see us bonding over what I assumed was a passion of his. I recalled the tutorial David unknowingly provided at lunch as I studied how he clipped the cigar and placed the torch to it and worked at the inhale-exhale routine to get the affair on with a proper burn.

Five minutes into the only quiet time I've had since chatting with David at lunch, Eden invaded my space as she stepped out to take a call. She never knew the difference between using her inside voice or screaming as if she was on a roller coaster ride, so when she laid into the caller in Farsi, I knew that she would finish, and I'd have to hear one of her grand stories of some far off place that her and Daniel had just returned from and how much better life was for those who didn't have all the responsibilities that she had.

Without fail, she ended the call and sat at the chair across from me and immediately launched into a tirade about how inept her employees in the Vietnamese factory that they built are, because they can't figure out how to spell Supreme or Adidas. The moment I sensed she was inhaling, I interjected, "What did David tell you that he was doing when you ran into him in Botswana?". She blurted out, "He was in the diamond trade." "Is that what he said? Did you ask him directly?" I was shocked to find Eden in a rare moment of silence as her eyes searched the sky for an answer. "Well, when I told him that Daniel and I provided heavy machinery to companies that mined minerals, he said, 'Got to keep all those women happy with diamonds.' So, I assumed he was in the trade. Why else would he been in Botswana? After we caught up over coffee, we later saw him at the Minister of Commerce building." I knew that Eden's certainty had faded and the leaps of logic she had taken could have led her to only one conclusion, so I asked, "He was in the building?" Once again waiting as she consulted the sky, "Well, he stood near the entrance…but when we got out of the car, he crossed the street, and I lost him in the crowd."

Right as the confusion was beginning to peak for Eden, a call broke her trance. She answered and immediately launched into a monologue in Farsi, except for the English profanities. Then she rose from her seat and motioned for me to excuse her as she returned to the house.

I continued to inhale the tobacco, hoping that the lightheaded trance I was slipping into was a natural byproduct for a cigar smoker and not the result of smoke inhalation. I didn't know how much time had passed from the moment I closed my eyes and began a breathing routine, hoping to get fresh oxygen flowing in my head, but when I opened my eyes, David was sitting across from me, firing at a cigar. A devilish smile covered his face as he released a plume. "Lightweight, you'll be okay."

David didn't seem fazed by the crowd, even though he hadn't had more than two minutes of evasive conversations with most of the people in the 25 years since high school. I wondered if anyone got more out of talks with him than the shaky assumptions Eden had made from her time with him in Botswana. I asked, "You okay with the inquisition?" He shrugged his shoulders, "I'll answer any questions they have, except the ones they shouldn't know." No smile, no hint he was joking - just a dead stare.

"So that's it, you're going to blow out of town?" I asked. David looked around the backyard at the bikes that were stacked next to the barbecue grill and then to the floatation devices that covered the pool and then back to me, saying, "I think I'll stick around."

My curiosity as to what "stick[ing] around" meant to David caused me to lurch forward as I questioned him. I asked, "How does that look David, sticking around, what will you do for work – what have you done for work, with your life over the years? David gave several inhale tugs at the cigar and then let out a plume through his nose and leaned forward, starring me in the eyes, "Paul, you should've been a prosecutor instead of a documentary filmmaker." "Cut the shit, David. Are you a hitman, a thief? What is it with you? I imagine you're flush, your dad left you with a nice trust?" After saying it, I realized the fear I held for anything I said that might anger David had real reason to exist as I noticed, for the first time, David showed his disapproval for me.

David sat back, clenching his jaws, and said, "Paul, all I ever got from my father was a name. Everything in life that I've earned has been because of my back." I didn't want to add fuel to the flames, so I remained quiet, hoping he would reveal more. "That Great War that I was talking about, well, I started fighting it early, many years before my father tried to guide me into his profession. He wanted to make films about military operations, and I knew that I wanted to be on the teams that carried out the task that he wrote about - the stories you hear about in bars - the stuff that never makes the news."

"So, you joined the military?" I asked.

"I joined a fraternity, not the DGA like you. My fraternal order gets Naval Crosses for a job well done, not Golden Globes. Failure for your profession means that you got snubbed with an Oscar nomination. Failure for me means that I get a star on a wall at Langley." David picked up my torch and added more flame to his cigar that has died out.

"Did you go in right after high school?" I knew that this was the most information that he had offered into his life and yet I still didn't have a clear picture.

"Paul, I know that you're a filmmaker and the next story exists around every corner, but mine has already been told. Just watch any flick with John Wayne, Jimmy Cagney or any bang-bang shoot'em up. So, yeah, my dad gave me that – the spark to strike out and do it my way. Best gift you can leave in a trust, is knowing you raised a sceptic." David's lively eyes had returned, and as I searched for the correct words, I was starting to puzzle together an image.

"So, no college for you?" I asked, hoping an answer would fill in the years. David pulled on the cigar and exhaled and paused, as he contemplated how he would tell me his story.

"Let me tell you about the very rich. They are different from you and me – actually, they are just like you. They possess and enjoy early, and it does something to them, makes them soft where we are hard – not so much you - and cynical where we are trustful." I sat as David took me through his view on the rich and what he saw as a life that he wanted nothing to do with, unless he built it for himself. As the story gained speed and the calendar years turned, I noticed the group had migrated outside and the box of cigars had been passed around, causing the thick smoke to blanket the table we stood around. Surprisingly, David continued.

The spiritual war that David did battle with would lead him to the Marine recruiter office in the Westwood Village on his 18th birthday and sign a three-year commitment. While in basic training, superiors identified his marksman skills and forwarded him to advanced training where he excelled and joined the ranks as a Scout Sniper.

David's skillset allowed him to be attached to a unit during the Balkan Wars where he earned a Silver Star for valor in combat; his team captured several warlords. He debated telling the part of the story where he was credited with killing two combatants with one shot. The possibility of a franchise with the story prompted Liz to ask for details of the scenario and David gave a quick, yet succinct lesson on trajectory, downhill force, distance, and how the weight of a round had to be accounted for when regulating your scope. By the time he got to the bullet hitting the combatants, everyone sat with the attention that is afforded to a celebrity at an acceptance speech. We had all forgotten that we were listening to a story of two humans being killed.

David's storytelling brought us to the day he had the decision to re-enlist for a five-year commitment or enroll at UCLA. He decided he would accept university studies as a break from killing and obtain a bachelor's degree in mathematics in under two years. Hearing that he was at UCLA, Eden blurted out, "You didn't reach out to any of us, and you were in LA?" David lowered his head in mock shame as he playfully submitted his hands to be lashed while laughing with the group.

I asked what he did after UCLA. David picked up his story from the summer of 2000 by backing up to his time in Bosnia at the end of the Balkan wars, where he was attached to a peacekeeping team made up of NATO allies. He was approached by a US Congressman who knew his grandfather. The Congressman was with a delegation and had invited him to join him for dinner on the base. David realized that the dinner was actually an interview to be an agent for the CIA while carrying out his duties as a Marine.

"How does that work?" Dan chimed in, as everyone else awaited the answer.

David chose to give the history of the Marines or as he referred to "his alma mater". The wars that Mariners fought from the halls of Montezuma to the shores of Tripoli is why the CIA usually taps individuals to act as counterintelligence agents to ensure that the chain of command is upholding democracy and not practicing it. The group was stunned to know that the CIA maintained uniformed agents on nuclear submarine vessels unbeknown to the commander or the rank-and-file servicemen.

By the time David had brought the group up to his CIA interview, I noticed that Liz had inched closer to him to hear every nuance in his tale, never once blinking her eyes.

"After finishing my studies at UCLA, I started my training at Langley." Once David confirmed that he was a CIA agent, Eden shouted, "So, that's why you were secretive in Botswana?" David replied, "You don't want to know what I was doing in Botswana." This caused Eden to form her hands like pistols as she imitated guns being fired. David winked in reply.

David's tale of training allowed Liz to chime in about her work with the CIA for the film *Zero Dark Thirty* that she produced. David's only response was, "Everybody loves to be humbugged." Dan came to her aid by saying, "It paid for the Malibu house."

David brought the group up to his first day with the CIA: September 11th, 2001. The mention of that day caused everyone to respond with varying degrees of shock. David paused, allowing us to collect our thoughts and share stories of what we were doing when the attacks happened. Maria commented how she had just hung up from a conversation with me, wishing me well as I prepared to board a flight from Boston to Los Angeles and how she was filled with terror not knowing that the plane that I was scheduled to board was the plane that was high jacked. I had missed my flight. The thought of this day causes tears to form. We decided to break for drinks.

I felt a sense of toughness by association. Aside from Eden, who had a 10-minute interaction with David in Botswana, I had several occasions to report. Those occasions, coupled with me being his everyday friend all through school, afforded me the rare opportunity to embellish my level of communication with David. When David took the group through the years, and some interjected, I remained silent and took a step back from the group to create the appearance that I was allowing the group their moment to catch up on an adventurous life I had intimate knowledge of.

David and I stayed outside while everyone else retreated to the warmth inside and I saw an opportunity to bring David up to speed regarding the lies I had told to the group over the years. "David, do you remember when we talked about your CIA time when we were in Antwerp?" He knew what I was pushing him towards. "I understand." That's all he had to say to soften my nervousness in having to retract stories that could expose me as a first-rate fibber.

"What was Antwerp about?" I asked. David paused, gritting his teeth before continuing: "I wrote a book. A fictionalized account of a group of CIA agents who pilfered duffle bags of US Currency that was meant to pay off Afghan war lords." I lowered myself into my seat and David followed, knowing he had my attention as he continued, "The agents use the funds and purchase diamonds, some raw, but all untraceable. The agents spend the next 10 years creating a network of corporations and accounts in foreign banks to introduce the funds back into the US once they walked away from the agency." I butted in, saying, "A laundry service connected throughout the globe. I can dig it." I knew using *Starsky and Hutch* vernacular would allow David to relax and continue.

"While the agents were exchanging stones, they came in contact with a black-market dealer whose life they monitored. During the dissection of his profile, they uncovered a heist that the black-market dealer was a part of, but instead of exposing the crew, they took down the score for themselves."

I believed that even without my fib, I was the one friend that knew the most about David, so when I recognized the stare David had employed, it was his way of advising me that this fictional tale of sanctioned thieves was not, in fact, fiction. "I'm Paul and you're David. You let me read your dad's *Playboy* magazines every month, and you didn't charge me like you did everyone else." "Can you dig it?" David said with a devilish grin, "It's dug." And with that, fist bumps sealed the knowledge that his novel was actually a memoir.

Feeling comfortable, David continued, "The agents bypassed a lock with 100 million possible combinations, infrared heat detectors, seismic sensors, magnetic fields and other sci-fi sounding measures which protected the vault that was three stories beneath the ground in a building that had cameras that covered every piece of lint that blew in its direction. The agents were unpacking stones in the hillsides of France by the time the authorities were alarmed to the heist that was reported to have insurance claims upward of $150,000,000."

I knew about the heist David was referring to. A gang, led by an Italian gangster, was arrested. David sensed that I had a question and stopped me by saying, "We are the CIA. If we can't find a fall guy, then no one can." And with that, I sat back in my seat and brought my hands together in a dramatic, slow clap, just as Liz returned.

In a tone that was removed of excitement, I turned to Liz, and asked, "Are you interested in purchasing the rights to the greatest thieves that you will never believe existed – who has never been captured, mainly because no one know that they exist?" Liz responded, "And this is why you are a documentary film maker and not directing *007* films; no passion, sell me on the story."

David saw it proper to interject, saying, "I wrote the novel." Liz's eyebrows perked up, "Why fiction?" David response was simple: "Statute of limitations are a fickle bag of laws." Liz shook her head showing that she understood as David added, "Life is always more interesting than fiction, but in this case, the tag 'fiction' will have to suffice."

Liz pulled a card from her purse and handed it to David, saying, "I smell a franchise. Do you have an agent?"

FIN

ROOM 104

Jacob ascends the steps of the one building that until now, he has only heard about in the dankest corners of the dark web. The building has become known as a place where people went and disappeared; sometimes the lucky ones eventually emerged with a new identity. Once he reaches the top step, he pretends he is tying the laces of his shoes so he can see if he has been followed. The street is empty, save a row of parking enforcement cars that lined the curb with the meter maids standing in a circle, calibrating their hand-held machines that print out parking fines.

One last scan of the street and Jacob swings open the glass door and steps into the building where he realizes he interrupted the beginning or the end of an affair with the participants unaware that he is sharing space with them.

Jacob considers how best to alert the thick-bodied black woman and the rail thin security guard who, at this point, is palming the right hemisphere of the lady's plump buttocks with his left hand. With the two of them lost in the moment and their back to Jacob, he decides to back up to the door, dragging his feet so the rubber soles of his shoes will make a screeching sound against the stone floor and alert them to his presence.

Jacob's ploy works, and as the lovers turn, Jacob keeps his head down, pretending to study his phone to sell the idea that he is not aware of their embrace.

"Can I help you?" The black lady's southern drawl rings out.

Jacob continues to view his phone, only raising his head as the lady calls out again, "Can I help you, Sir?"

"I'm sorry, I didn't see you," Jacob replies, and for the first time he looks at the lady who, for a split second, shares a resemblance with the smiling face of the Aunt Jemima syrup lady.

"I reckon you didn't hear me either. You here for The Center?" The lady asks.

Jacob nods as the lady waves for him to come to her as she retrieves a clipboard that sits on the security guard counter.

"You Jacob Price?" the lady asks.

"Yes," Jacob responds, as he fights against the urge to not stare at the collection of hairs that line lady's chin.

"I'm Ms. Jackson and this is Mr. Alvarez. When you come in, check in with Mr. Alvarez and make yo way to room one-o-pho."

Jacob nods as if he understands the instructions.

"Do you understand?" Ms. Jackson asks.

Masking his desire to laugh by lowering his head, Jacob responds, "Yes, check-in and go to room one-zero-four."

"One-o-pho. Room one-o-pho. Down that hall," Ms. Jackson says, as she pointed down one of the two options that exists, then adds, "Go that way. Don't ever wander off and go down that haw. You got no biznes down that haw."

Jacob nods as he looks at Ms. Jackson and then turns to Mr. Alvarez who stares back at him, with a bushy mustache that covered his mouth until he releases a half-hearted smile that reveals two silver caps where his front teeth would ordinarily be positioned.

"Buenos dia," Mr. Alvarez greets Jacob, as he motions with his head towards the hallway that Jacob was told was off limits. Then he says, "No camines de esa manera," as he points to the restricted hallway.

"Si," Jacob says, as he exchanges awkward grins with Mr. Alvarez.

Ms. Jackson interrupts the smiling standoff when she says, "Well go ahead. I be in there shortly to check-on ya'll."

Nervously, Jacob repeatedly bows his head at the two of them as he takes a step back and then to the side which allows him a clear path around the desk that Ms. Jackson and Mr. Alvarez stand at. Once he is about to enter the hallway that leads to room 104, he stops and looks back, where he witnesses Mr. Alvarez resuming the squeezing of Ms. Jackson's backside.

Jacob hurries down the sterile hall, stopping when he comes to the door that is marked 104. Before entering, a thought comes to mind, and he backtracks his steps to the doors he had passed and notices they aren't marked with numbers. The sound of Ms. Jackson laughing rattles any thoughts Jacob held of investigating the unmarked doors and instead, he proceeds to room 104 and enters.

Peeking inside room 104, Jacob scans, starting from the front of the room where he sees neatly lined rows of school styled chair-desks. His eyes take in the view, only stopping as he catches the stare of the man who looks to be sitting for the painting of the middle-aged version of *Dorian Gray* – replete with thick wavy hair that has turned gray decades prior, spectacles that sit on a Romanesque nose and a chin that can withstand a buckshot at close range. Upon seeing Jacob take steps into the room, the man stands, tossing his newspaper onto the table, and in a hushed tone says, "Welcome. Bienvenue. Come in, close the door."

Jacob steps into the room, and notices a large chested girl dressed in cut-off jean shorts that highlight her toned legs. The girl appears to be freshly out of her teen years as she dons a Justin Bieber T-shirt that she has tied in a knot in the back, causing her shirt to rise, revealing her jeweled navel ring. Jacob forces himself to not stare. She concentrates on her phone as she mimes words, while twirling her blonde hair with Lolita-like seduction.

"What did they stitch you up for Son?" the man asks, snapping Jacob back to the moment where he sees the man extending his hand that Jacob meets with his.

"I'm sorry," Jacob responds, prompting the man to take him by the shoulders, guiding him to the chair next to his.

"Have a seat. I can see you are in the denial phase. First timer. Your handlers told you not to talk about it. That it'll all blow over and you'll be back in circulation in a month or two. Right?" Jacob appears confused at the man's statement.

"I'm Fredrick Douglas. Yes, named after the great abolitionist. Irish heritage. Some say that we are the Negroes of Europe and therefore my parents recognized the spirit of Mr. Douglas and, well, they figured bestowing the name on me, I'd learn who he was, and his life work would serve as a well for me to draw from, throughout mine."

Jacob continues to nod his head and adds, "Has it been?"

"Every Irish parent waits with bated breath not knowing if the child will be stricken with the Irish curse of pale skin, freckles and a carrot wig on top. So, in preparation, a name with some provenance is the cheapest gift that you can give a child. I was fortunate to evade the curse in this life, but, as you can see, the other curse of the Irish caught up to me and here I am, a drunken fool, serving out a sentence."

Jacob nods his head and adds, "That's amazing. Pleasure to meet you, Fredrick. Jacob Price. I'm Jacob Price. Um, it was my grandfather's name. Um, he fought in the war, so I never met him."

"Excellent. The Great War. Now, what did they get you for? Why did you get sent to the gulags?"

Jacob lowers his head in embarrassment as he struggles to respond. Finally, he says, "It's a long story."

"Lay it on me. We aren't going anywhere. I'll tell you what. I'll give you, my offense."

Just as Fredrick begins to talk, the girl from the back of the room steps forward and says, "This is going to be a long one. Ole Silver Fox can talk."

Jacob stands to greet the girl who extends a fist that Jacob meets with his as he says, "I'm Jacob."

"Laura, but you might know me as L-Bad Ass."

Jacob looks to the ceiling as he considers the name. "I'm sorry, I can't place it."

Laura sits on the desk behind the row that Fredrick and Jacob are in, smacking at Jacob's arm to gain his attention as she speaks: "Last year, I had gone viral from a video where I was doing the Dougie at a Lakers game. Bam, overnight, a million followers on IG. Kylie Jenner paid me to model her lipstick. NBA dudes falling over themselves, sliding in my DMs shooting their shot. I had DJ Khaled working on some songs for me."

Jacob interjects, "Wait, I remember that Dougie video. I don't get what happened?"

Talking through a smile Laura continues, "I'm at a Kendrick Lamar concert down in Miami, and he called me up on stage to sing 'M.A.A.D City.' You know the song?" Laura asks Jacob.

"Yeah, If Pirus and Crips all got along…Yawk! Yawk! Yawk!"

Laura bobs her head to an imaginary beat as she adds, "All good up to that point..." Laura stands, modulating her voice as she reenacts a performance, "… and I go, "Man down. Where you from, nigga? Fuck who you know, where you from my nigga?"

Fredrick interjects. "I think Jacob understands. You sang the lyrics to the song Mr. Lamar wrote. The song that Mr. Lamar recorded, called you on stage to perform as he had performed plenty of times before that night."

"That's what I'm telling him." Laura adds.

"It's just the word is so vile, no matter who is saying it."

Laura leans close to Fredrick as she holds back the tears that are seconds from flowing, "But I am now called the racist for singing the words to a song that a black man wrote and that I bought. Help me see how that's fair."

"It's not. Welcome to 2021. You are now in The Center where you will stay off that phone of yours, where I'm sure you were on Twattle or

Snick-Snack-Chat or something and they will find out and you'll be extended."

Laura says, "Like you?"

"Yes, like me. That Irish spirit refuses to conform. I'm a rebel woman."

Laura and Fredrick share a laugh and a fist bump as they turn their attention to Jacob, waiting for him to add to the conversation.

"That's fucked up. Seemed like Kendrick sandbagged you."

"More like tea-bagged me," Laura says with a laugh.

A devilish grin covers Fredrick's face as he considers the thought. "Now that is a sight."

Laura playfully slaps at Fredrick's arm then says, "Tell him the stupid shit that you got sent here."

Fredrick clears his throat and says, "I am a tenured professor of literature at Harvard University. For whatever reason, I foolishly engaged in a conversation with a group of students on reparations to descendants of slaves in America. I reminded the students that I am Irish and that unlike many African Americans today who can't trace their heritage back to a slave, I can. My great-great-grandfather was recorded as an Irish slave on a ship that landed in America. If there are reparations to be distributed, then I too want in on it. That didn't sit well with the busybodies on campus who looked for racism in every glance."

With a perplexed stare, Jacob asks, "Is that it? Isn't college where open debate happens?"

"Oh, you poor fool. You speak like a Neanderthal. Campuses are where axes are grinded, and careers are on the chopping block."

Just as Jacob is searching his thoughts for another question to ask, the door swings open and a group of college girls, dressed in softball uniforms, steps in. The lead girl looks around and asks, "Is this where we make statements?"

Fredrick stands to answer and quickly sits down as he hears Ms. Jackson's voice, "No. No. No. Go two doors down the haw. That's where you go to make statements."

The group files out of the room, leaving Ms. Jackson's figure taking up the space. Jacob doesn't turn his head fast enough and is now locked in a stare with her, with Ms. Jackson adding, "Mr. Price, I'll be back with some forms for you to sign." Then she closes the door.

Jacob turns to Fredrick, who has his attention fixed on the newspaper. He turns back to Laura, who pretends to be focused on the newspaper that sits on the desk. When he looks back at Fredrick, he asks, "What is the deal with her?"

"She worked at the DMV before the state opened up these centers," Fredrick said in a matter-of-fact way.

Jacob shakes his head and says, "I could smell government bureaucrat like it was cheap perfume. Who were those girls?"

Laura walks to Jacob and adds, "Listen, when Ms. Jackson comes, pretend you're reading something. They don't want the inmates to talk amongst one another. They put a stack of approved newspapers up at the front and that's what they want us to read."

Jacob stands and walks to the table at the front of the class where he thumbs through the papers, letting out a chuckle as he reads out loud, "the *New York Times,* the *Washington Post*, and the *Tribune.* Come on."

Fredrick chimes in, saying, "State approved. All parts of the machine. By the way, those girls are, or were, on the Fresno State Softball team. They refused to take a knee during the National Anthem. If they keep to their guns with that defiant spirit when they go to the statement office, they will tell the national press to piss off. If that happens, they will be assigned to Room 104."

Jacob considers Fredrick words and ask, "How long have you been here?"

"Nine months. My third rotation," Fredrick says with an air of pride to his words.

Appalled at what he just heard, Jacob walks back to the seat next to Fredrick and asks, "How do you pay your rent. How do you buy groceries?"

Fredrick laughs at the question which further confuses Jacob and then says, "Cancel insurance. Geico offers it in an umbrella plan."

"What the hell is that?" Jacob asks.

"Just how you have unemployment insurance if you get laid off, cancel insurance is now offered."

Jacob asks, "What if you can't afford it?"

With deadpan delivery, Fredrick says, "Welfare. Simple. There is a bill before Congress now called the "Woke Insurance Initiative" and they want to mandate employers to offer cancel insurance as a part of an employment package, where it's a part of the FICA tax."

Jacob looks to the ceiling as he tries to process what he is hearing when Fredrick asks, "What was your offense?"

While Jacob considers the question, Laura takes a seat on the table, awaiting a story. Jacob releases the pent-up air and says, "I used to be a writer for Dave Chappelle."

"No shit!" Laura interrupts to the chagrin of Fredrick who shushes her.

"Yeah, I've worked with Dave for years. My process is simple. I work on new material by going out to little comedy clubs in small towns and I don't submit to Dave until I've left the crowd killed over in laughter. Well, that used to work before everyone started filming everything. Now, I hang out in the neighborhoods and work through routines with guys that play the dozens, your mama jokes, anything. Offensive isn't a word in their vocabulary. The most creative, raunchiest shit you can say wins."

Fredrick interjects, "Yeah, yeah, yeah, cut the fat, get to the meat."

Jacob issues an awkward smile as he continues, "One Latin kid hit me with a lame recycled joke about white guys dick sizes and I unleashed a barrage on him. I ducked down and screamed out, 'La migra! La migra! La migra!' Here is Francisco. Followed it up with a good ole question and answer set-up: 'Francisco, what's the best thing about dating your homeless mother?' Everybody around asked, 'what?' and I said, 'you can drop the bitch off anywhere.'"

Laura and Fredrick break out in laughter as Jacob continues, "Francisco, what's the difference between a joke and three dicks? Francisco, your mom can't take a joke! I followed it up with another: What's the difference with Francisco priest and a pimple? The crowd asked, "What?" The pimple didn't cum on Francisco's face!"

"These are all strikes in the game, right?" Fredrick asks.

Jacob pauses as he considers the question, with tears starting to form in his eyes, he adds, "All strikes in the game, yes, but some asshole recorded it and put it on Twitter with the hashtags: racist-white-guy-demonizes-Mexican. Racist-white-man-attacks-POC. Misogynist. Sexist. Homophobic. Transphobic. Oppressor."

Laura says, "They hit you with shotgun blast. Did Francisco step up?"

"No. He said that he couldn't. Someone online put together a GoFundMe account for him under the guise that he had PTSD. They raised over $100k. He said if he spoke up then he wouldn't get the money."

Fredrick clears his throat and adds, "And here you are, on your first cycle. Cancel insurance young man or get ready to go hump it on an oil rig in Montana."

The three pause and then grab newspapers and pretend to be reading them as they hear footsteps in the hallway. The door opens and a tall black man dressed in black slacks, and a gray cardigan with brogue shoes steps in, pausing as he looks at Laura, Fredrick and Jacob.

The man says, "I was told to check into room one-zero-four. Is this one-zero-four?"

Jacob cracks a smile and replies, "Yes, The Center, but are you sure they said one-zero-four? This is for folks who have been…"

The man says, "Cancelled. I know. Yes, I was cancelled."

Laura, Fredrick, and Jacob stand and walk towards the man with confused looks, with Fredrick speaking for the group, "Why?"

With much pride in his words, the man says, "I'm a black Conservative."

Fredrick nods his head as if he understands and says, "Grab a newspaper. We're getting acquainted."

*****

Erin Liebowitz walked down the marbled hallway on the 20th floor of the Cantor, Fritz & Marsden law offices. She had yet to complete her first month with the firm and was still familiarizing herself with the building and all the personalities that exert power in workplace politics. Erin knew that her fair skin that freckled easily when exposed to the sun and the curly hair that looked like she had a freshly minted perm had served her well as it didn't allow anyone to place her into an easily identifiable ethnic box. She didn't present as black or white, nor did she demand to be viewed as either. Erin knew that no matter which ethnic group she identified with, she would be judged more harshly for what people assumed she should act like based on who they thought she should be. For that, she had perfected her diction with annunciated words that appealed to any English speaker from either coast, which further served as a roadblock for anyone who wanted to define who she was.

With the gate of an athlete in her prime, Erin's slender frame was highlighted with a smart pantsuit as she arrived at her destination where she saw the title for: Evelyn Jamison Office, Human Resource Coordinator. Erin looked at the placard bearing Evelyn Jamison's name and playfully strummed her knuckles at the door that was ajar. "Come on in." Erin heard the Southern accent of what sounded like an annoyed woman coming from inside the office. Erin peaked her head in and took in the sight of a dreadlocked woman with the smoothest mahogany complexion that she had ever seen. Erin took note of the woman's hair that was fashioned in an upswept tail that allowed anyone viewing to take in her sharp facial features that were fighting for attention with the feathers that dangled from her ears and the colorful stones that made up the necklaces that rested on her buoyant breast.

Erin stepped in the office and headed to the woman with her hand extended only to be startled as the woman's voice barked orders, "Have a seat. I'm Evelyn Jamison and you are?" Erin guided herself into the chair that was positioned opposite Evelyn on the other side of the desk.

"Erin Liebowitz. I received an email from you." Erin replied in a matter of fact, resolute tone as she realized that she had encountered a less than hospitable host.

Evelyn stood up, revealing that she was wearing a linen maxi dress that clung to her curves. Once fully erect, Evelyn stared at Erin, lowering her voice to a whisper, "Listen here. You got the whole high-yella thing going on, and that might get you into the Yale Club or out of a speeding ticket, but let me tell you, batting your hazel eyes at me won't get you far, sistah."

Erin's confusion grew as she searched for a proper response to what was turning out to be a bizarre encounter. Knowing that she had to say something, Erin attempted to speak and formed a word that turned into a stuttering response, "I. I'm. I don't understand what is going on. Did I offend you?"

Evelyn interrupted, "You think you aren't black."

"Is that a question?" Erin responded.

"Well, are you black?"

"Why am I here? What does my ethnicity matter?"

"Why doesn't it matter to you?" Evelyn responded, jutting her neck out in Erin's direction, adding, "You gonna learn."

"Learn what? What the hell is going on?"

Erin noticed that Evelyn's neck had retracted and the scowl that covered her face had receded. The aggressive tone had given way to a cheerful, high-pitched affected voice, "Hello. Mr. Cantor, this is Erin Leibowitz. Have you two met?"

Erin turned to see Mr. Cantor, a towering figure whose rotund upper body pushed the limits of his ill-fitting suit. Erin stood and exchanged handshakes with Mr. Cantor.

"Erin, I'm glad you've met with Evelyn, she is like the heartbeat of this place. I'm sure you two have a lot to talk about." Mr. Cantor said, causing Erin to turn back to Evelyn who now had a smile glued to her face.

Evelyn interjected, "Yes, Erin, that's why I called you in. I have put together a program for our staff, a program that has been praised by several studies for leading the charge in providing racial sensitivity training in corporate America."

Mr. Cantor added, "We are not saying that you are racially insensitive. It's just, if we have all of our employees go through the program, we can highlight that to potential clients."

Erin's attention went from Mr. Cantor to Evelyn who maintained her smile then added, "Evelyn, you created this racial sensitivity program?"

Talking through her smile Evelyn responded, "Yes, well, here at Cantor, Fritz & Marsden. The program that you will attend incorporates our program. Don't worry, the firm will cover the cost and your week in the program is counted towards ongoing studies."

Mr. Cantor extended his hand to Erin that she met with a firm shake then he added, "Take any advice that comes from Evelyn. She has her finger on the pulse."

Hiding her confusion, Erin responded with a simple, "Thank you."

Erin watched as Mr. Cantor exit the door and then she turned to Evelyn whose resentment had returned to her face as she directed her words to Erin, "You better get with the program. My program. This patriarchy is not going to go for it too much longer, so, while they pretend to be all into this equality talk, get what you want."

Erin chuckled and asked, "So, is that what you are doing, using guilt to exert what?"

"Reparations. However it comes. The program you are going to, my auntie runs it. Nice government contract. Now, you better figure out if you are black or not?"

Erin looks at a form that Evelyn shoves in her direction while speaking in a muted tone, "The people love to be humbugged."

Evelyn inquired, "What did you say?"

Erin looks up from the paper and smiles as she responds, "I was wondering what happened with the circus now that all the animals aren't in the show. I figured it out."

*****

Erin sits in a chair, focused on the pages of the *New York Times* she has laid out on the desk. Sensing that she is being watched, Erin turns and catches Jacob, Fredrick, Laura and Alonso as they lower their heads into the newspapers and magazines on their desks as they pretend that they aren't watching her.

"Come on, that's just weird."

Jacob stands and walks to Erin while pleading with her, "You got to give us more than what you've said. It doesn't add up."

"That's all I have." Erin says.

"Your law firm sent you here for racial sensitivity courses. But what did you do?" Fredrick asks.

"The law firm that I work for. Yes, they said that I stay for a week course, and they get to tout that they are a leader in the industry."

Fredrick stands beside Jacob, rubbing his chin, just as Alonso steps forward, "The grass is getting thick. They are now preempting cancellation."

Jacob ads, "So if you run afoul of the PC agenda, they can fully cancel your ass because you've already been given the playbook."

"That's sneaky. That's how they won't be liable with the insurance companies," Fredrick says, causing Erin to search the clouds for a question.

Erin asks, "Insurance companies. What are you talking about?"

"There is a whole racket to this Room 104 sensitivity training shit. I was ahead of the curve and purchased cancel insurance at the University where I work. But, if what you say is correct, and believe me, I don't doubt you, their next step is to have us so out of options that all we can do is comply." After making the statement, Fredrick is resigned to the idea. He turns on his heels and walks back to his desk where he sits and considers the possibilities.

"The grass has gotten really thick," Alonso says as he laughs while walking back to his seat.

Laura stands up, and makes a beeline to Erin where she asks, "You're black?"

Not allowing her frustration show, Erin answers, "Is that a question?"

"Yeah. I mean, you look half-and-half of something. I just don't know what. Leibowitz. That sounds white."

"It's a garden variety Jewish name. My father is Jewish, from South Africa, and my mother is a Jew. Her parents are black and German," Erin says matter-of-factly.

From his chair, Alonso shouts out, "Big ups to my African sister in the front. I'm Dominican and black, but if the cops say, "Freeze Nigga!" I'm gonna freeze like an ice cube."

The room breaks out in laughter as Alonso walks back to Erin's chair. He says, "You are being sent here is your company's way of putting you on notice. We all did something, or so they say, but you, they let you know that they have got the power to silence you if you don't dance to their tune.

Jacob nods as he says, "Yeah, we all violated the thought crimes. But, if I'm not mistaken, then what they will be doing next is not saying what you can't say, or that what you say is offensive, but even worse, what you must say so that you are not offensive to whomever is a member of an aggrieved group."

Alonso issues several guttural sounds then says, "Checking off boxes. I got dick-in-the-culo treatment because I spoke out against all the "inclusive" dog-and-pony show bullshit which they say is meant to give voices to underrepresented writers in Hollywood. But when you actually do a deep dive into the box checking, if you only check off two boxes, then someone that can check off three or four wins."

Laura thinks about Alonso's statement and then ask, "But you are black?"

"Is that a question?" Alonso says before he and Erin let out light laughter.

"Yeah. You're black, so isn't it all about giving POCs a shot at opportunities that have been closed off, where white guys like Jacob are writing jokes for Chappelle and shit?"

Alonso raises his index finger, placing it to his temple as he answers Laura's question, "That's what they say. They have tricks in their pockets and props up their sleeves like a stage magician. They give you the illusion -- the appearance of truth. As a writer, I just want to give you the truth in the pleasant disguise of illusion. These motherfuckers have handicapped me with their bullshit equality push."

Once Alonso finishes his statement, Laura asks again, "But, aren't you black?"

Jacob turns to Fredrick who has stood from his desk with Jacob waving him to enter the conversation.

Fredrick clears his throat then says, "Laura. I mean, L-Bad Ass. Intersectionality provides a ladder of importance to the busy bodies who pretend to be concerned about equality. If you are a straight white male, then you are at the bottom, unless you are already at the top in your profession, where none of the busy bodies that set the rules are stepping down off of their perch."

Alonso lets out a soft clap as Fredrick takes a breath, and ads, "Can you dig it?"

"It's dug," Fredrick responds, prompting Fredrick and Alonso to exchange fist bumps as Fredrick continues. "Now, a straight black man or POC of any variety is one-step above, with women above them. I don't have a joke to add, but I should. It actually writes itself. Where was I? Okay, here I go. If the woman is lesbian, then she steps ahead. If she is transitioning, then she steps further ahead on par with a man who is similarly situated."

Jacob interjects, "A POC male only has two boxes to checkoff."

Containing his frustration, Alonso adds, "And that's why I got cancelled. I dared to exercise my right to freedom of speech."

"Freedom of speech has its limits when in the workplace. Look at Kaepernick," Erin says.

Alonso paces in front of the classroom, tapping his chest with a clenched fist as he responds, "I beg to differ. Kaepernick thrusted his anti-police stance onto the fans. 'Pigs in a blanket, fry them like bacon' slogans. He went Huey Newton and whipped up those in the streets that held grievances and the moment that he got a payout offer, he mysteriously went silent. Plus, he was a third rate QB whose career was on shaky grounds before all of that noise. He only extended his time in the public square. I dared to offer the comparison in an op-ed with *Deadline*."

Erin allows her intrigue to show, saying, "I read that article. Well written."

"Well, I'm a writer. It better have been well-written."

The group hears the clanking of high heels approaching the door, causing them to hurry to their seats where they pick up the newspapers that are on their desks. Erin looks around the class and locks eyes with Fredrick, who motions with his head for her to focus on her newspaper, just as the door opens and Ms. Jackson steps in, "How ya'll doing today?"

The room responds, "Beautiful day… lovely day."

"That's good. I'm going to leave ya'll with a work package to take home. We have got a lot to cover in the next week. Critical Race Theory. The 1619 Project. America pre-Columbus and the Trail of Tears. Ya'll gonna see. It ain't gonna be pretty. So, put your privileges to the side. That includes you, Ms. Leibowitz and Mr. Rodrigues. Ya'll too have privileges akin to the white men in this class."

Unable to restrain himself, Alonso asks, "What privileges do I have?"

Ms. Jackson eyes Alonso as he continues. "Maybe some of ya'll need to recycle the course. Maybe all of ya'll need to recycle. Your privileges are engrained. Ya'll take a package as you leave out for the night. Let's end with a pledge."

Erin watches as the class stands to attention, which prompts her to rise as Ms. Jackson leads the class in a statement: "Lift every voice and sing. 'Til earth and heaven ring. Ring with the harmonies of Liberty: Let our rejoicing rise…" Ms. Jackson pauses as she consults her thoughts for the words as the class awaits. Seconds pass and Ms. Jackson abandons the notion and tells the class, "Shit, I forgot the lyrics. Ya'll go on now. I'll see you tomorrow."

FIN

GEORGIE PORGIE

Cradling a cigar in his massive right hand, George stood on the jagged, broken glass-filled rocks that line the parking lot between the Malibu Beach Inn Hotel and the Malibu Pier. A cigar on a Sunday night after finishing a chapter of his novel had become a weekly reminder that the next day was the beginning of a new week, and the clock was ticking for closing out the next chapter.

George was in the 44th year of his life. Thirty pounds have been added, where he proudly labeled himself a stout man since he had officially become a professional writer, 15 years ago. His salt-and-pepper goatee fit well with his utilitarian style clothes. If he hadn't paired with the tortoise framed glasses and Rolex watch, he could've been mistaken as a lumberjack. Up to this point, he hadn't challenged himself by finishing a novel. He had plenty of ideas for novels, but usually he turned them into short stories or screenplays, where had he not been compensated and the adoring press not showered him with praise, he would've been forced to challenge himself and go well beyond the twenty-thousand-word count that made up his longest short story.

This week, George's journey to enjoy his cigar at the ocean wasn't to mark the end of another chapter, but to commemorate the typing of the word *FIN*. George had finally finished his grand novel. Even with four of his 40 short stories that have been published in the *New Yorker* magazine, later adapted to films and three produced as plays, his *New York Times* bestselling memoir about his experience sitting with Fidel Castro in the last year of his life, the finishing of a ninety-eight-thousand word novel was to him, the breaking of any jinx he had assigned to not having written in the only form that he deemed the realm of bonafide writers – the novel.

Cigar smoking was a habit George adopted when he turned 40. Throughout his 30s, alcohol was a constant companion of his – a habit that resulted in the depletion of his savings to pay legal fees from the D.U.I.s he had accumulated after looking for story inspirations at the bottom of a bottle.

Cigar smoking provided George the calm that he reasoned was fitting for a man in his 40s. It also was a welcome distraction for him as he knew that he had transferred one potentially deadly vice for another. Where he risked insulting friends or strangers while in a drunken rage, with his new hobby as a cigar smoker, he could only offend a passerby who got caught in the heavy smoke if he didn't judge the wind properly. Mentos and spearmint gum on hand helped reduce the risk of offense to anyone that was meant to be in his space. As much as he wanted to chew on a couple of sticks of his favorite, Big Red gum, he didn't want the reminder of the drunken nights where the cinnamon taste overpowered the alcohol that had soaked his tongue.

He removed a Partagas series D. Robusto from his leather humidor case. For his weekly journey to the ocean, he was certain to have at least three cigars in his travel case, and that his torch lighter was filled with butane gas. He usually ignored a cutter as he preferred - as he was doing - to bite off the cap head of the cigar and chew on it, while he toasted the foot of the cigar with an even distribution of heat. The grin on his face after spitting out the plug of tobacco was his way of saying, "come to daddy" as he took in the first draw, causing the cigars foot to shine lights of a siren.

After several puffs in, George heard in the distance the giggles of lovers who were exiting the only car, which was in the parking lot that lined the rocks that he stood on. A tall, shirtless teen boy exited the car, revealing his muscular backside. The teen's shorts were falling at his waist, as his naked female companion made her way out of the car where she noticed George starring at them, causing her to hurry into the backseat of the Toyota Rav4 while pulling her shorts up, ignoring that her shirt had fallen to the ground.

The shirtless stud picked up her clothing and tossed it into the backseat, then closed the door. George turned to face the ocean as he was well into enjoying his cigar. From his peripheral George saw the stud walk to the rocks and light a cigarette. With 30 yards between them, they stood on a parallel line. George continued his inhale-exhale routine as he turned to face the shirtless stud who issued a head nod as he flicked his cigarette out at the ocean, then turned and strutted to his car and entered.

George's eyes followed the stud as he started the engine, which engaged a techno beat that rang out from the speakers. The stud gunned the car in reverse, slammed on the brakes, which caused the car to roll a few feet as the transmission adjusted to forward drive, where George watched the car speeding towards him, before the stud turned the wheel towards the exit, allowing George to catch a glimpse of the shirtless girl covering her face as they passed. George released a plume of smoke as the car sped onto PCH as he said to himself, "well done young man."

Within seconds of the stud speeding onto the streets, a Highway Patrol car raced eastbound on PCH in the direction of the couple. The red lights and wailing of the siren were George's cue to turn back to face the ocean as he chuckled, wondering if the patrol car was headed to stop the stud's car and if the girl would be able to put her shirt on before the officer caught up to them?

Traffic on PCH in Malibu after nightfall allowed enough time for turtles to cross without hassle, so when a car passed with a revved engine, pedestrians took notice. Sounds competed with the crashing waves of the ocean, but when the screeching of brakes broke through, accompanied with the wailing of a horn like the BMW that had pulled to the side of PCH, George was forced to take note.

He didn't have to search for the car, as it was the only one in his eyesight on the side of the road. The occupant of the car hadn't exited, but after 10 seconds of laying on the horn, she had sat up in the seat. He continued to draw from the cigar as he awaited what would happen next. A thin-framed woman emerged from the car, dressed in a black blouse, with a form-fitting pencil skirt. The woman's high heels that she managed to keep on made the stumbling walk laughable to George, even with the thought of a car passing and bulldozing her.

He focused closely on the woman's bronzed complexion and soft Oriental features as she held her phone to her face, screaming, "Why? Why? I love you!" George braced for impact, wincing as the woman made it to the center divider just as a Porsche honked the horn without breaking, just changing to the free lane as it raced by the woman.

George stepped away from the rocks in case the woman decided to abandon her steps to cross the eastbound lane. With each shaky step the crying woman took, George took three in her direction, but eventually stopped as the woman increased her speed, beating an SUV that passed as she stepped onto the sidewalk.

The intensity of the crisis that had been averted caused George to draw on the cigar with a longer than usual inhale. The long plume that he expelled revealed just how much smoke he had taken in, which was now clouding his vision. He fanned the smoke away and realized that he had lost sight of the woman.

Once his sight was restored, he noticed the woman was walking down the middle of the parking lot. He wondered if she had seen him watching her dodge the dangers of the road and was now avoiding him, but as her steps increased down the lot, and she hadn't turned in his direction, it was safe to assume that she didn't realize that he was present.

George remained motionless, resuming a normal inhale-exhale routine as he watched the woman approach the gates that lead to the pier. He began making bargains with himself. He concluded that the right thing to do was wait, and if she walked onto the pier, then he would give chase. What he would say once he made it to her wasn't fully worked out, he just knew that he couldn't allow her to stumble around the pier in the foggy state she was in.

He hurried his steps towards the woman just as she tugged at the locked gates of the pier, causing him to stop and wait at a trashcan.

Frustrated with the gates, the woman headed to the steps that lead down to the beach. George knew that the woman's high heels were no match for the steps that she was now descending. Whatever reservation he had in not wanting to interrupt her drunken mission, he knew that he had to make himself available if she needed him. George resumed his motion in her direction and picked up the pace to a jog. Once at the top of the steps, he adjusted his sight where he noticed in the darkness, the woman on her knees, continuing her cry into the phone, "why?" He had a dilemma. Not wanting to invade her moment of grief would have to take a backseat to his knowledge of the tide that had a set plan that didn't bargain well with thin framed drunks, no matter how expensive their high heels were.

From the top of the steps, George called out, "Ma'am. Are you alright?"

He cringed at the thought of sounding like a man from another era as soon as the words left his mouth, but the woman hadn't responded, so he added, "I'm going to stay here. If you need me, then please tell me."

The edge of the tide washed over her body, leaving her to search the skies for answers, but only to find George standing at the top of the stairs. For the first time, the woman's gaze acknowledged George as her cries resumed, followed by tears.

Tears began to form in George's eyes as he saw the face of a gamine who wasn't sure about what her next decision was going to be. He was certain that he had to act, or she would be lost to the sea.

"Ma'am, my name is George. I'm coming down to help you."

With his cigar secured at the corner of his mouth, George hurried down the steps, taking note that the woman was struggling to stand as another wave came in, covering her up to her waist, eventually throwing her back to her knees, just as he made it to the last step where he grabbed a hold of her with his right arm, while holding the rusted out metal rail with his left, pulling her to him, in a death match with the sea. Finally, acknowledging that her life was in jeopardy, the woman held onto George as she screamed, "Help me!"

George maintained his grip as the water retreated, which allowed him to lower the woman to the sand, where he stood over her, allowing himself a second to adjust his thought. His cigar still affixed in the corner of his mouth, George looked up at the next wave that was building momentum and knew that they didn't have much time to waste, so without consultation, George scooped the woman up and climbed the stairs.

Reversing the count of the stairs that he had descended, George knew, without seeing, that he had two steps left to the top, so he lowered the crying woman down and then removed his cigar from his mouth and was pleased to see that he managed to keep it dry. Before looking down at the woman, he took one long inhale, pointed his head to the sky and blew out the smoke, watching it travel out to sea and returned to the crying woman that laid at his feet.

"Thank you," the woman said repeatedly through her tears, with her voice trailing off to a whisper.

"You don't have to thank me," George responded, locking eyes with the woman as he adjusted himself off the last step, bending down, placing his face within inches of the woman, who didn't seem bothered by the cigar smoke as he secured both hands in her armpits, where he guided the woman to an upright position.

"Alright, here you go. I'm George," he said, leading her to a bench. "What's your name?"

"I'm Birdie."

Hearing the name, George chuckled as he repeated, "Birdie." Then he added, "Well, Birdie, with all that tumbling around you did down there, you didn't let that phone go."

Birdie looked down at her phone and laughed through a cry as she held the phone and said, "Priorities."

George took another inhale of the cigar, then tossed to the side what was now little more than a nub, then he pointed to the space next to Birdie on the bench and cautiously said, "I'm going to sit here."

"You didn't have to do that. I like the smell."

George considered Birdie's words as he mouthed a silent count to three, then added, "I'm going to sit here and if you want to talk, I'll listen."

Birdie nodded her head that she understood as she eyed George who had retrieved his cigar case from his shirt pocket, "Just a cigar" George added, biting into the cigar cap, while searching his pockets for his torch lighter.

Intrigued with George's routine, Birdie asked, "Why did you bite it?"

George placed the torch to the foot of the cigar that was cradling in his hand as he chewed on the plug of tobacco, turning to Birdie, and adding, "At every stage in the making of this cigar, a human hand was involved, in the same tradition from centuries past. To honor the hands that picked the tobacco, separated the leaves then those who fashioned this particular cigar for me to enjoy, I don't think it would be proper to introduce a machine to invade the process."

George noticed that Birdie was eyeing him, so he extended his hand, offering the cigar that she accepted without contemplation. "Do not inhale," George warned.

"Well, what do I do then?"

"It's not like a cigarette. Draw in the smoke and hold it in, swish it around so you can taste it, then, release it," George said, as he pointed his head north with his lips pursed as if he was whistling.

Birdie placed the cigar to her lips and attempted an inhale that she fumbled as the smoke filled her face, which causes her to cough as George interjects, "No. No. No. You're pushing out. Put the cigar in your mouth, wrap your lips around it then draw on it."

George's instructions elicited a smile from Birdie, with her adding, "As you wish."

Birdie opened her mouth to form an O-ring as she turned to face George while guiding the cigar into the open space. George realized he was nodding his head, agreeing with her as Birdie secured her lips to the cigar, where she drew in for a count of three, with George saying, "okay, hold the smoke…now roll it around, then release it. Blow it out."

Following his instructions, Birdie released a stream of smoke that extended several feet into the air. "There you go," George said, as Birdie admired the cloud that she created as she placed the cigar to her mouth, repeating the process before handing it back to George.

"I think I'm getting lightheaded." Birdie said while bracing herself on the bench while trying to evade the smoke-filled air.

"Cohiba," George said with a devilish grin as he inhaled from the cigar.

"What is that?" Birdie asked as she wiped her eyes in an attempt to clear her vision.

"When Columbus arrived at the New World, he sat with the Native Chief. The Natives that assembled were smoking tobacco from a pipe and several began to go into a trans-like dance, believing they were seeing spirits. Columbus asked what it was they were consuming, and the Chief said,"Cohiba". A couple hundred years later, Castro popularized the name Cohiba for cigars and used them as gifts, handing them out to ambassadors he was trying to win over to his cause."

Still bracing herself on the bench and continuing an inhale-exhale routine, Birdie asked, "Did he tell them what to do when they got lightheaded?"

Talking through a smile as he stood up to face the ocean, George said, "You're doing it. It'll pass."

Seconds go by before Birdie broke the silence saying, "Thank you for helping me."

George acknowledged her with a head nod, allowing Birdie to continue saying, "I'm in a bad head space. I think you can tell." Birdie stopped as she considered her words.

"Tell me what you want me to know," George said, as he continued to look out at the ocean.

"I came here to die. Well, I was hoping to convince him. Well. I have to tell you the back story," Birdie said as she stood facing the ocean, shoulder-to-shoulder with George. She continued with her story. "I've been having an affair with a man I work for. He lives here in Malibu. He says that it is over, for no reason. Well, he has a reason, he's married, with two kids. I'm also drunk. I've been drinking."

"I know that you've been drinking. I saw how you hobbled across PCH," George said, which allowed the two to share a laugh.

Birdie continued her story as she fought back tears, saying, "he said he wasn't going to see me anymore. I came out here to see him. I went to his house, and he wasn't there. He is in Santa Barbara with his family." Unable to finish her story as her voice cracked, George extended his arm. Birdie tucked herself at his chest.

Seconds passed and Birdie added, "I was going to jump off the pier, but the gates are locked. Then I went down the steps and I figured I'd walk into the ocean." Birdie paused with the thought of what she had done as George asked, "Well, can you swim?"

Birdie looked up at George and laughed. Then she said, "I'm actually a good swimmer."

George looks down at Birdie and said, "Aside from looking like a wet cat, you survived, and your phone made it intact."

Birdie's eyes filled with tears as she cleared her throat and said, "I called my mom and she said she is booking me a flight to come home."

"Where is that?" George asked.

"Manhattan. I leave tomorrow morning at nine."

"Will you return?"

Freeing herself from George's embrace and walking back to sit on the bench, Birdie said, "Yes… I don't know." George eyed Birdie, sensing she had more to say. "I don't want to go to my place tonight. He leased it for me. Then, without me knowing, he leased the unit next to me to keep an eye on who I had over. For months, I didn't know he was keeping tabs on me. A fucking stalker."

George lowered himself in the space on the bench next to Birdie and offered the cigar that she accepted, working through the inhaled routine that she believed she has perfected, as George said, "This adult thing isn't easy."

While releasing the smoke a thought came to mind for Birdie, "What are you doing out here? Oh my god, maybe you have a family that you have to get home to."

Hoping to calm Birdie, George shook his head and said, "No. No. No. I'm right where I needed to be. No one is up waiting for me."

A frown covered Birdie's face as she asked, "No wife or girlfriend?"

George imitated Birdie's frown and said, "Nope. No."

Birdie handed the cigar back to George as she began to convulse, while holding her hair back into a tail with one hand as she said, "I'm going to throw up." A concerned George stood, and realized that an explosion was imminent, he took a step away from Birdie who had gone into a squat position, where she attempted to run away from George as a stream of vomit flowed from her mouth.

George stood at a distance and allowed Birdie to expel the contents of her stomach, then he asked, "Is that all?"

With sweat beads covering her forehead, Birdie managed to laugh as she responded, "Dinner: Yes. Lunch is still in there. Don't worry, I survived four years at Pi Phi sorority. I'm a professional."

George's eyes travelled from Birdie to the vomit and back while letting out a whistle, then adding, "You got some distance. That is pro level projectile. And you're a hearty eater."

George's comment made Birdie laugh, as she looked up at him and shifted to a matter-of-fact tone as she said, "That's for the week."

"I'll get you a water out of my car," George said as he walked away.

"Hold on. I'll come with you," Birdie said as she stood up with her eyes closed while performing a breathing routine that looked to George like it may cause her to faint.

"You going to make it?" George said, as Birdie flashed the okay sign.

"All good," Birdie said, as she walks towards George with long decisive steps showing that she had regained control of herself as she passed George, adding, "Where is your car?"

"No doubt, you are a pro," George says as he picks up his pace, catching up to Birdie.

"I do thank you for helping me. If you don't have any plans, and there isn't a wife and kids waiting up for you, maybe you want to pull an all-nighter with me," Birdie said, in a coquettish tone that caused George to consider what it meant by "all-nighter".

"Sure. What do you have in mind?"

"I haven't thought that through. Your call," Birdie said, as she reaches for George's cigar that sits in his mouth.

"You just emptied your stomach, so food would be the go-to right now."

Without breaking stride, Birdie inhaled the cigar and rolled the smoke around in her mouth as George instructed and then released a cloud that trailed behind them as they covered the parking lot, adding in a question to George, "Where?"

"My old haunt, Swingers," George said while chuckling, which caused Birdie to question him, "That's not what it sounds like, is it?"

"No. It's a diner on Beverly. You could benefit from the meatloaf plate," George clarified.

"Are they even open now?" Birdie asked, as she hands the cigar back to George.

"I've mended many broken dreams there. The meatloaf plate always does it for me," George said, as he points to his car, a 1977, British racing green MG soft top that was parked in front of the Beach Inn.

"Here we go," George added, as he opened the trunk of the car.

"This is your car?"

With much pride in his voice, George said, "Yeah. This is the first car that I ever drove. Well, not this one. I got this one from a guy who lived in Bakersfield about a year ago and I've tinkered with it here and there."

Birdie inspected the car with suspicion as she said, "It's a convertible."

"Yup. What will you have?" George asked while holding open the cooler that sat in the trunk, revealing water bottles, Johnny Walker Blue label liquor and several Red Bull energy drinks.

Birdie eyed the selection and said, "Somebody travels prepared. I'll take the Red bull."

"Good choice. Me too," George said, as he retrieved two Red Bulls, handing one to Birdie.

As Birdie opened the Red Bull, she asked George, "Listen. If you're married, then let me know. I can't be involved in any way with more bullshit."

Without opening the door, George climbed into the driver seat, looking at Birdie as he started the engine, he said, "This is the only lady in my life."

Birdie followed George's lead and climbed into the car, lowering herself into the passenger seat where she was puzzled as she searched the car for a shoulder strap seat belt, just as George leaned over to her and pulled at the waist belt, securing her in place.

Once George secured Birdie, he tossed the cigar that they shared onto PCH and then he reached over her to open the glove box and retrieved a case he opened, revealing a row of cigars. The two sit in silence as George removes a cigar and repeats his routine of biting at the cap then torching the foot of the cigar. One long inhale from George and then he passed it to Birdie who accepted, then with a devilish grin she said, "Georgie Porgie, Pudding' and Pie, kissed the girls and made them cry." Just as Birdie stopped at the word "cry", George added, "This Georgie don't do any running." Birdie's grin gave way to the cigar she placed in her mouth as she eyed George who had started the car. It caused the engine to rev before he shifted into gear and jutted onto PCH.

***

George maneuvered the sports car down the winding road as birdie enjoyed the night air that whipped her face. Sensing that she hadn't probed into George's life, Birdie asked, "Why cigars?" Shrugging at the question, George responded, "There are worse habits one could have." "Name them," Birdie said. "Kleptomania," George said. in a direct tone which caused Birdie to erupt into laughter before adding, "Not at all. I'd just go to Tiffany's with an excuse if I got caught."

Birdie reached for the cigar that sat between George's lips, unaware of the flimsiness of the ash that had formed. Her tugging motion caused the hot ash to spill onto George's arm and thigh. Birdie immediately begged for forgiveness, as she wiped George's pants. George briefly took his eyes off the road as he looked at Birdie who realized that she was brushing his inner thigh. "I'm so sorry," Birdie said. "It's okay. Mistakes are the prerogative of young ladies." Birdie was taken aback by the comment and playfully taunted George with the cigar. "Not the same mistakes," George added.

Birdie sat back pulled on the cigar and looked out at the ocean to her right and then turned back to George and asked, "How old are you?" "44," George said, as Birdie looked back to the ocean in thought.

"That's little blue pill territory, right?" Birdie asked.

"Thankfully, not for me. A Red Bull is all I've needed. Why?"

Birdie didn't answer George, as he noticed she was consulting her phone, which alerted him to focus back on the road. "Andrew. That's the guy. He didn't want me to know that he swallowed Viagra, but I knew. I knew when it hadn't kicked in yet." Birdie finished her statement and then transitioned back to her phone.

"Everybody has a story. My mother pushed; I came out. She fed me; I grew. I'm here now," George said, in a tone that showed he was annoyed. Then he added, "You're not over this guy. It's too soon. That's alright. And he isn't over you. Take a beat. You'll figure it out."

"Sage advice," Birdie said as she stared at George and then she added, "Tell me more."

George considered what he wanted to say as he shifted gears to slow the car as they reached PCH and Sunset Boulevard where he turned left. "Born and raised in LA. Parents divorced when I was 10, so on Fridays, after school, I rode the RTD from my mother's one-bedroom apartment in Koreatown, to be with my dad who lived in Century City. In a city with all this diversity, on that bus ride down Wilshire in the 80s I was able to see that although we breathed the same air, it was like the two parts of town were as different and far away as the moon is from the earth."

"How so?" Birdie asked with sincere interest.

"Koreatown was as real as you could get to a melting pot with immigrants from Asia, South America, and the Caribbean. All at or below the poverty line. The Mexican gangs were locked in their war with each other, so with me being bused to a school in the Valley, I evaded a lot of the hassle because I was on the bus before they rolled out of bed. But, after school, all the crazies were out: Gangsters, wannabees, crackheads, street vendors. Name it. And they walked the streets. My bus stop was a block from my mother's apartment. She was a teller at the bank, so I was a latch-key kid. I'd pop a frozen pizza in the microwave and do my homework before she got home."

With curiosity in her voice, Birdie interrupted, "What is the RTD?"

George allowed a laugh as he responded, "the Rapid Transit Department or the Richard T. Davis as we called it. Acronyms. It's what the Metro was before it was the Metro."

Birdie nodded and snuck in a peek at her phone before adding, "When did you see your father?"

"After school on Fridays. I'd already have my bag packed, and as soon as I'd get home, I was back out the door. A straight shot down Wilshire. That's what I mean, on that ride, all the housekeepers and nannies that worked on the west side were who I shared that bus ride with. By 4 p.m., all the laborers were in their trucks going east and I was headed west, like we were switching sides. The difference is I'd go to stay overnight, and they were just visitors in the world I got to occupy from Friday until Sunday night."

"And then?" Birdie asked while looking at George, who was unaware she had turned her attention back to her phone as he answered her question.

"Well, then my dad remarried, Alana. Nice lady. She has two kids, Fredrick and Francis. Frick and Frat, still to this day, my annoying little stepbrothers. My mom moved to West Hollywood and my dad got a house in Brentwood. It's like the further west she moved, the further west he went to keep a couple of miles between them."

George glanced at Birdie and noticed she was holding her phone and focused on a message that she was texting as she responded to him, "Like he was running away?"

Birdie's response informed George that she was able to multi-task, which allowed him to shift his eyes back to the road as he continued, "No. But, that is what he joked about. Enough about me. Where are you living in LA? Where does your kind party?"

Birdie lowered her phone and rambled off cities: "Beverly Hills, Hollywood, Echo Park-Silver Lake area mainly, but I'll go wherever the action is." Birdie resumed her texting. George was shocked, saying, "Knock it off. Echo Park-Silver Lake. All the way up to the mid-2000s that area was a war zone and now girls like you hit up bars and clubs without fear."

Without looking up from her phone, Birdie said, "Gentrification. The gift and the curse I suppose."

While shaking his head to say, "whatever," George expelled the sucked-in air, creating a pucker whistling sound and then added, "I suppose so. My mother moving to Hollywood was in her estimation a step up from Koreatown because of the status that was conferred on her from friends back in Ohio. Just because she lived in Hollywood with the movie stars, but she knew that the mental geographic barriers that separated the east – Hollywood – from the west side – Beverly Hills and on – she hadn't made any progress. You had to be west of La Cienega and North of Pico to be considered a success."

Lowering her phone, Birdie said, "I don't see that. I went to SC with plenty of rich kids."

"Students, yes. They put their time in and don't stay, well, at least they didn't years back."

With a grin, Birdie said, "But this is like in prehistoric times, like before cellphones."

"Yeah, the days when you jingled as you walked because of the quarters in your pocket to use the payphone. Times have changed. It is now trendy to party in Echo Park without concern that you will be a mark by some Vato Locos hoped up on dust."

Birdie consulted her phone, awaiting a message to arrive while asking George, "Where did you go to college?"

"RISD."

Birdie erupted in laughter as she said, "You're a Scrottie. I'm shocked."

George joined in on the laughter with less exuberance and with a straight face said, "I had a blast."

"Draining your Scrotties?"

Birdie continued her laugh as George pointed to the cigar in his mouth, and said, "I can't hear you." Then shifting his hand to draw her attention to the sign that reads, "SWINGERS" in cursive lettering, he said, "We have arrived."

"Maybe they have meatballs on the menu, your alumni," Birdie said with a straight face, followed by George imitating Birdie in a mocking tone: "Maybe they have meatballs on the menu."

***

Birdie stood off to the side of George, focusing on a message she is reading as George gets the attention of the waitress that has tattoos that fill every space of her body that wasn't covered by the uniform that Swinger's waitresses are known for: combat boots over knee high socks, black high-waisted short skirts with a form fitting Swingers logo T-shirt – brassier optional.

Birdie lowered her phone when she realized George was facing her with his outstretched arms for her to follow the waitress to the outside seating, "Is all okay?" George inquired.

"Yeah."

"Your mother?" George offered, as he sensed Birdie wasn't going to provide any further information.

"Yup" Birdie said, shaking her head as the two sit at a table.

George pretended not to be interested in interrogating Birdie, as he realized that throughout the car ride, she had vacillated from being a free-spirited companion to becoming preoccupied with a text exchange, so instead, he focused on the waitress' name tag: "Sharon. Meatloaf dinner for me, with a large Coke."

With a less than impressed expression glued to her face, Birdie eyed an uninterested Sharon who was looking down at her note pad, while balancing her gum in her masticating jaws as she asked, "And you honey, what will you have?"

"Fuck it. The same. You only die once."

"Eat here for a week straight and you might change your mind," Sharon said, with a smile as she removed the menus and asked, "You want a Coke with that?"

Birdie nodded. "Thank you."

George waited for Sharon to enter the diner then leaned over the table towards Birdie. He said, "Be careful or Sharon will tell you the story behind all of those tattoos.

Birdie said, "You see the legs and arms on her? Somebody doesn't miss her CrossFit class."

"Every waitress here has that corn fed vigor to them. It's a prerequisite to employment. Two layers of bondo, 10 tattoo minimum, and at least 3 restraining orders on record," George said in a low tone as his eyes shifted from a wide-eyed Birdie who was sitting on his every word to a medium-framed man who was dressed like he has been sleeping under a bridge with his grungy jeans, turned up cowboy boots and T-shirt replete with holes throughout. The man didn't break stride as he recognized George.

"How are you, George?" he asked, extending a clenched fist that George meets with his.

"Shia Labeuf has emerged. Good to see you man," George said, as Shia slowed his pace, allowing his companion, a tall, thin-framed man who was dressed in a pink mini skirt and cropped toped T-shirt that exposes his toned abs. As the man caught up to Shia, he adjusted his blonde wig that sat off-center several degrees on his head.

"Hello beautiful people," he said to George and Birdie, as he accepted Shia's waiting hand. Once Shia had a grip, he guided the man to a waiting black SUV, depositing the man in first, turning to George as he closed the door, "We should get together soon. I'll call you."

George watched the SUV drive away and turned back to Birdie, who was staring at her phone at a text that said: THE UBER IS COMING FOR YOU. COME TO ME.

"Did you see that?" George asked.

"Yeah, Shia Labeuf, an actor, is sneaking around with a crossdresser. Isn't this LA?" Birdie said, in a less-than-interested tone.

"He was in a movie that I wrote. I had no idea that he would cross the train tracks like that. Damn," George said, and then added, "I don't usually care, but I wonder how the paparazzi will report this?"

With a confused look, Birdie asked, "Paparazzi who?"

George points to a Hispanic man across the street from Swingers that was dressed like a Navy Seal with cargo pants, boots, and a windbreaker. He cradled a long lens camera in one hand and a cellphone in the other.

"He is calling his news desk now to let them know he has caught a whale," George said.

"I have to use the restroom," Birdie said, as she rose, unable to look at George who attempted to show chivalry by standing as she walked away. Realizing he was standing alone at the table; he took his seat.

George pulls his cellphone from his pocket and typed into the search: IS SHIA LABEUF GAY? He began to scroll through the various articles, unaware that Birdie bypassed the entrance to the diner and instead, continued down the street, going from a fast-paced walk to a jog to reach the gray Prius that was waiting with the hazard lights blinking.

Birdie entered the car and slumps into her seat where she took a deep inhale as the round-faced, bespectacled driver caught her eyes in the rearview, inquiring, "For Beatrice?

"Yes," Birdie responded, as she lowered the window.

George looked up from his phone, just as Sharon returned to the table carrying two plates filled with hearty portions of mashed potatoes, carrots and two thick cuboid shaped pieces of meat. "Are you going to eat both of these plates?" Sharon asked.

Confused with the question, George didn't respond, causing Sharon to ask as if George was hard of hearing, "Are-you-going-to-eat-both-of-these-plates?"

"She just went to the restroom."

Sharon chuckled, "That little chicken-legged girl hoped into a car a second ago. This is all on you."

Scoffing at the thought that he has been abandoned, George's eyes rose from the two plates Sharon placed on the table before him, then he said to himself, "I'm not surprised."

FIN

A COW, A CAT & A HORSE

WANTED: THREE ESCAPED CONVICTS

1. Alvin Coolidge, 5'9", 160 pounds, blonde hair, blue eyes
2. Choi Lee, 5'5", 130 pounds, black hair, brown eyes
3. Leroy Jackson, 6'2", 230 pounds, black hair, brown eyes

Choi, a rail-thin Chinese man with a shock of greasy curly hair, which he wipes from his eyes every time the wind changes direction, sits nervously behind a ten-foot haystack in the horse barn on Farmer John's property. Alvin, the stringy haired blonde who looks like a back-up singer from Ram Jam – bell bottom jeans included - approaches Choi, pulling him to a gap in the haystacks that Leroy, the mahogany-skinned hulk, is peeking through.

"Choi, you gotta see this. Leroy, step aside," Alvin says, while tapping at Leroy's massive shoulders.

"Lordy Lord, I will run through that like a hot knife through buttah," Leroy says, while whipping drool from his plump lips.

Alvin guides Choi's face to the opening, directing him where he wants his attention, saying, "Look."

Choi squints, as he focuses on the image of a curvaceous blonde who is in her room in the main house. Once the image is clear to Choi, his mouth falls open as he studies the blonde, who is sitting at a vanity mirror, brushing her wavy hair.

Turning to face a smiling Leroy and Alvin, Choi mangles the English language, saying, "Alvinnn, all de place-we-hide, you choose farrrrhm where daughtah is butie queen."

"What I tell you? One hour with her would be worth going back for another dime," Alvin says, while rubbing the whiskers, which make up his goat-tee.

"Brutah, why didn't we keep running? We could've been clear to Tampa by now?" Leroy asked.

"Exactly. We are less than a mile from that hell hole that I led you two out of. Not to mention the hounds that are out looking for us. They think that we are way in Tampa by now, never imagine that we are right next door," Alvin says, thumping his index finger to his temple, which causes Choi and Leroy to have an ahh-ha moment.

"You fucking genius. I'm going to get some pussayyy now. We got time," Leroy says with excitement filling his voice.

"No. No. No bruthahhh. Your big gorilla-looking ass is going to scare that white girl if you go climbing up into her window. I'll go and prime the situation. Plus, Choi and I can't get in any trim after you. I've showered with you for the last five years and have seen that Alabama swamp water snake that you got. We would need seat belts, so we don't fall in if we go after you. I'll go first," Alvin says to Leroy, who is beaming with boyish pride after hearing the compliments.

Alvin creeps from behind the haystack barrier the three are hiding behind, tiptoeing around farming equipment that litters the barn where he makes it to the rickety door that he eases open then steps out. He looks back at a smiling Leroy and Choi who congratulate him with thumbs-up signs.

Full of confidence in his mission, Alvin turns back to the curvy blonde who is now standing at the window, enjoying the breeze that has her nightgown hugging her body. The thought of what he is going to do once he climbs up to her window has taken over Alvin. He is no longer cautious with his steps, unaware of what is before him, and just as he returns to his path, he becomes aware of the feeling of his boot-catching metal, and a split-second later, the wooden end of a rake smacks him in the face, causing him to scream out, "Fuck!"

Farmer John appears at the back door in a ratty checkered robe over long john underpants, with a shotgun in hand, "Whose there? I'll kill you!" he says, as he chambers a round.

Unable to make it back to the barn, Alvin hides behind a roaming cow, thinking the only way that he will stay alive is if the next sound that the farmer hears has to be convincing, so he opens his mouth and says, "Mooooooo."

Farmer John eyes the cow, unaware that Alvin is hiding behind it, accepting that the cow is just mooing, as cows do, and turns on his heels, back into the house.

Choi turns to Leroy and says, "Alvinnn, not guuud-on-foot-like-me. I go now."

Choi bypasses the equipment as Alvin had done, steps to the left around the rake that thwarted Alvin's mission, tapping Alvin on the shoulder as he passes him, whispering, "I let you know how blondie smells."

Unable to see much beyond five feet in the darkness of the yard, Choi doesn't realize he has stepped on a cat, causing the cat to dart around the house, bumping against the gate, which alerts Farmer John who reappears with shotgun in hand, "Whose there? I'll shoot you dead!" Farmer John says while chambering another round.

Hugging Alvin behind the lone cow, Choi let's out the walling sound of a cat, "Meooooowwww."

Farmer John walks back in the house while mumbling through a laugh, saying, "Damn cat. You almost got shot."

Leroy stands at the barn gate, chuckling, as he watches Choi and Leroy locked in an embrace as they hide behind the cow, knowing that it is his turn to make it to the curvy blonde who has sat back before the vanity mirror, resuming her hair brushing routine.

"I'm going to split her into two pieces," Leroy says, as he pushes open the barn gate, walking with all the confidence of a free man, passing Alvin and Choi on his journey, unbothered with the land mines that exist in the yard between the barn and the house. "Watch me do my thang my main Honky and my little Oriental friend," Leroy says, looking back at Choi and Alvin just as he reaches the stairs, where he climbs, step one, two and three with one remaining, and just as he puts his weight down, his boot bust through the rickety wood causing his leg to disappear up to his knee.

Leroy hears Farmer John's running towards the back door and knows that all he can do is lay flat, closing his eyes hoping that his black skin blends in with the darkness of the night. Farmer John pushes open the door, chambering a round as he screams out, "I know someone is out here. Come on, show your face. Who is there?"

Knowing that he will be shot dead if he doesn't convince Farmer John that he isn't an intruder, Leroy clears his voice and says, "It's the horse."

FIN

TRIMALCHIO IN WEST EGG
The characters originally appeared
in F. Scott Fitzgerald's *The Great Gatsby*

Dressed like he was playing the part of a banker in a bespoke three-piece pen striped suit, with his hat in his left hand as he nervously brushes back into place loose hairs that have fallen onto his face with his right, Nick Carraway stands next to Henry C. Gatz. Unlike Nick, Henry's attire of a simple wool suit lends one to believe that he is comfortable with tossing his jacket to the side and rolling up his sleeves for work at a moment's notice.

Henry eyes the non-descript silver urn that sits on a podium, next to an over-sized photograph of Jay Gatsby, who is dressed in a white suit, and balanced with his slick-back black hair that frames his tanned skin and soft eyes that connect with the viewer, inviting them into his world.

Nick stumbles with his words as Henry clears his throat, cutting off Nick as he says, "You did well Nick. Every detail as he prescribed."

"Just as he prescribed," Nick says.

The two men turn to face Pastor Tobias, who is approaching from the back of the church.

"Mr. Gatz, Mr. Carraway, I will be here all day if you want to return. If anyone comes later, I will receive them, and if need be, I will repeat my eulogy for one, or for a group, if a group assembles," Pastor Tobias says with the intent of conveying calm.

Staring past Pastor Tobias, Mr. Gatz's eyes come alive as he steps forward, with his arms open as he receives a man who seems to have stepped off the photograph, alive and full of youthful vigor. "My son, Lazarus," Mr. Gatz says, holding back tears.

Nick leans into Pastor Tobias and whispers, "You are not witnessing a miracle. Mr. Gatsby was a twin."

Pastor Tobias's eyes scan Lazarus from head-to-toe and then he turns and examines the image of the man on the photograph, turning back to Lazarus where he says, "If we were in another era, I would say that our savior is back in the land, working his craft. You gentlemen can take as much time as you need. Lazarus, my apologies for not knowing. Your brother was a man of honor. His gifts to the Lutheran community guarantee his name will live on for many years to come. Please excuse me."

Nick steps to the side as Pastor Tobias walks past him with a puzzled look to his face.

Lazarus extends his hand to Nick who receives it with care as the two men pull one another closer into an embrace. Lazarus whispers to Nick, "You did well young man."

Nick holds the embrace and replies, "Of all the names, Lazarus is the most fitting.

Lazarus places his arm around Nick and guides him on a walk to the entrance of the church when, once in the doorway, he pauses and looks out at the empty parking lot. He says, "Only Owl-eyes, huh?"

"The old man had to see for himself that Jay Gatsby was dead," Nick says.

"What's in the urn?" Lazarus asks.

"Ashes from your fireplace. Sand from the West and East Egg. I was tempted to mix in some cinnamon," Nick says, as he walks in step with Lazarus and Mr. Gatz.

"I got a kick out of the name. Jay, I mean, Lazarus. How long are you going to keep this up?" Mr. Gatz asks.

"Until day is night and night become day. Or, until the music stops playing," Lazarus says.

Mr. Gatz collects himself and then opens his arms, receiving Lazarus for a long embrace. Once he steps back, with his eyes locked on Lazarus, he says, "Jay…Lazarus, if it gets too much to handle, or too little, you can always come home."

Lazarus cups Mr. Gatz face with his palm, replying, "I know. Thank you."

Mr. Gatz turns to Nick and extends his arms for a hug, which Nick accepts. Once fully composed, Mr. Gatz says, "If I had two boys, I would've wanted the other one to be just like you Nick."

Humbled by Mr. Gatz's words, Nick lowers his head, nearly bowing, as he holds back tears. Once he raises his head, he notices a procession of cars passing the church. Packard's, Cadillacs, Rolls Royce's, and several men on motorcycles race down the road.

"Someone is having a party," Lazarus says.

***

Lazarus sits in his leather chair behind a grand mahogany desk in a dimly light study. Just as Nick enters, Lazarus stands, pretending that he is looking for an unknown item. "I'll get the light," Nick says as he switches on the Tiffany lamp.

"Nick, I hate to admit this, but my memory hasn't fully been restored," Lazarus says.

"I understand."

Lazarus eyes the paintings and books that line the wall, and then turns to Nick, saying, "I'm looking for the proper words, more than I am an actual item." As if a thought has come to him, he laughs as he sits to mask that another thought has evaded him. Recognizing Lazarus is lost in thought, Nick issues a comforting smile. The two pause the gay moment as the phone rings. Lazarus eyes travel up, meeting Nick, adding, "Well, let the games begin."

Nick allows the phone to ring three times before picking up the receiver. "This is Nick Carraway. How can I assist you?... Yes." Nick hands the receiver to Lazarus, who is now standing. Clearing his voice and issuing a wink to Nick, Lazarus summons a strong tone, "This is Lazarus... Hello Meyer... I understand you couldn't make it... Yes. Everything is just as it has always been done. I will phone you when I arrive in the city... Until then. Goodbye."

Allowing himself to breathe as he ends the call, Lazarus lowers himself into the chair in sync with the phone receiver being placed back in place. Lazarus clears sweat from his forehead, which causes Nick to ask, "Should I get you something to drink, maybe open the window?"

"No. I'm okay. Just getting my bearings," Lazarus says, just as Nick takes a seat in the chair, opposite him, lowering his elbows onto the table, attentive to a story he seems to be pulling out of Lazarus. "Okay, I promised, so I will deliver," Lazarus says.

"I am all ears." Nick says, as he flashes a quick smile.

"If my father didn't tell you, we are not Old Stok American. There wasn't any generational wealth. Yet, every man in our line knows his way in the land and sea. At 17, in 1907, I happened upon Dan Cody who taught me what to do with money once I made it. He had and enjoyed it, so I knew that he knew what he was talking about."

Nick says, "Your father says that you traveled on the yacht, Toulomee."

"I saved him. He invited me to stay and travel with him. I saw the world: West Indies, South America, Cape Town, well, I'll get to Cape Town shortly."

"South Africa. Compressed carbon," Nick says, prompting a nervous smile from Lazarus.

"Nick, it isn't often that I'm in a conversation with someone and they know what I am going to say…"

"Or what you're not saying," Nick says.

"Very well, I will cut the fat away." Lazarus says. "Mr. Cody left me an inheritance that his mistress, Ms. Kaye cheated me out of. A handsome fortune of $25,000. For a man of 22, that could go a long way or be squandered in one night playing the type. I didn't understand it at the time, but Ms. Kaye's theft did me a favor. Equipped with wit, charm and an experience that could rival the most intrepid explorer, I had to figure out what to do next. I had pent up anger. The US had just entered the war, so I enlisted. I became a doughboy. The truth is, I had lived so much life with Mr. Cody that I was okay with dying. I thought I was living on borrowed time as it was."

"But you didn't," Nick says, pointing to Lazarus, as he rises and walks to the liquor stand, where he pours bourbon into two glasses. "I would've accepted death. Youth… makes you do stupid things that some find heroic, but when you look back on it, you wonder why the man you shared the ship ride with is sitting in some mass grave with shrapnel stuck in his body and why you were spared. The guilt of surviving can haunt you on quiet nights."

Lazarus pauses, as he watches Nick on his return to the table, sitting down a glass in front of him. Nick takes a sip, while Lazarus sits himself side-saddle on a slither of the desk, and says, "I'm still here."

"Part of my anger derived from Daisy ignoring me throughout the war. Not one letter," Lazarus says, standing upright, which prompts Nick to stand, placing the two men to face one another with the desk between them. Fully alert and hanging onto Lazarus's every word, Nick sips his drink, with

Lazarus following. Lazarus continues, "I was at Trinity College and finally, she reached out to me to advise me that she had married Tom."

"It was a garishly designed affair. Without my sunglasses, I would've gone blind," Nick said.

Lazarus chuckles and says, "I heard." Then he pauses his story as he takes another sip from the glass and says, "I knew I had to return to the States with more than just an experience, that is, if I was going to win her to my side."

Nick sits and Lazarus follows his lead as he continues with his story. "Mr. Cody introduced me to a diamond exporter when we were in Cape Town. I once overheard him going on about his apartment in London and how he rarely stays in it, opting for the bed of his mistress in the countryside. I made my way over there and one night, I watched him leave and then entered through a window. I had hoped I had time to search every inch of the place, but I wouldn't need much. What I hoped to find was on his desk, in this satchel." Lazarus removes a black satchel from his inside jacket pocket and places it on the desk to an awe-struck Nick to examine.

"Was that the beginning of Jay Gatsby?" Nick asked.

"The stones that are in that bag was the beginning of the Jay Gatsby that people would respect because that's what the stones stood for."

"Didn't you sell them? How do you still have them?" Nick asks.

"I didn't have to sell them. I used them as leverage. I've been a savior, a student, an heir who was cheated out of what was owed to him, a doughboy, a mad fool in love, a thief and none of that mattered to those who took my money. No one asked the provenance. I was welcomed in."

"Why do you still have the stones?" Nick asks.

"I'm going to return them to the man, and I want you to accompany me on the trip."

Before Nick can respond, a knock at the door alerts the two. "Come in," Lazarus says.

The door swings open. A round-faced woman, dressed in a white maid's uniform, steps in and says, "Mr. Carraway, your guest has arrived."

Puzzled by the statement, Nick responds, "My guest. I'm not expecting anyone. Angela, who is it?"

"They said that they were late to the memorial services and that they went to the wrong church. They heard that Mr. Lazarus was here, and they wanted to pay their respects to the Gatsby family. Look." Angela points to the window, which prompts Lazarus and Nick to hurry to get a look.

To their surprise, the procession of cars they saw passing the church are all lining the lawn, with upwards of thirty people standing in their finest party attire.

Lazarus turns to Nick and says, "Let's give them what they came for. Tomorrow, we leave for London."

Nick turns to Lazarus, extending his hand that Lazarus meets with his and says, "I'm in."

FIN

DISPATCH FROM THE FRONT LINE

First appeared in the August 4, 2020, edition of The Artifactuals, an online arts and cultural magazine.

"Not Today Opie"

"The pitifulest thing out is a mob.; they don't fight with courage that's born in them, but with courage that's borrowed from their mass…" – Huck Finn, Mark Twain

I was driving east on Beverly Boulevard in Los Angeles with my dog Spanky resting on the passenger seat. It was a late-Spring Day, and I was approaching Fairfax Avenue where trendy boutiques sit next to skate shops and Orthodox Jewish markets. That's when it happened, one of those what-the-fuck-is-this moment: a wall of protesters had taken over all four lanes of traffic. They held signs that mirrored their chanting, "FUCK THE POLICE…BLACK LIVES MATTER…NO JUSTICE, NO PEACE!" Some cars ahead of me were able to move to the side of the road to let the mob through, but most, like me, were stuck, captive to whatever their next move was.

I inched ahead, trying not to hit anyone, but soon I was forced to a dead stop as the mob grew larger, and more vocal. Some had shifted their venom from generalities to insults directed at me. A lady began to shout into my window, "Don't you see us walking…move your fucking car…black lives matter!" "What do you want me to do," I answered back, "pick my car up likes it's a wallet and run away?" Before I could finish stating my case, I heard BOOM! BANG! BOOM! BANG! from the rear of my car.

I looked up at the mirror and saw a red-headed Caucasian male slamming on my trunk. I had no need to question his intentions, because I already knew what they were: he, like many protesters that afternoon, wanted to instill fear in anyone not marching in their direction.

"Not today, Opie Taylor," I uttered to myself, and moved into action.

*

I should note here that I'm Afro-Cuban, one of those whose lives presumably mattered to them. Who they believe is being hunted by the cops. I grew up in the Hancock Park area of Los Angeles, full of people with distinct cultures: Koreans, Philippines, Armenians, Russians, African Americans, Caribbean and a range of immigrants from countries south of the border. I ate their food, ran the streets with them, exchanged knuckles, then went back to one or another of their houses and played Atari or The Dozens. There was no diversity mandate. You clicked with a guy, or you didn't. Life goes on.

By the time I was 12, I was already a juvenile delinquent, doing delinquent shit, so when my Guatemalan buddy Eduardo got me a gig with him as a look-out for Turbo, a leader of the first generation, El Salvadoran gang, Mara Sava Thrucha, I hopped at the chance to get in on the action. Looking back, the pay was shitty and the weed they were selling was Mexican dirt at best. Today higher strains of it can be purchased in a dispensary without much hassle. Times have changed.

The cops we ran from were dealing with the drug and gang wars that were terrorizing the city. The areas and cultures that I daily crisscrossed also demarcated the Hispanic and black gangs that laid claim to the streets. I knew to tread lightly.

Several times a week I took the RTD bus to the boxing gym in Watts. In that bus ride I passed through at least 20 different gangs and never once was I afraid that I would be made to join them. I was into sports, and in my experience, the gangs didn't recruit. Some guys I knew in those neighborhoods pledged their allegiance to the gangs, and others did their own thing. The nightly news made gangs out to be blood thirsty heathens who preyed on the young to fill the ranks of their army, but that didn't square with what I saw.

During the 1992 riots, I was a sentinel for the Korean grocer whose store I worked at in the summers, stocking shelves. Just as the looting began, I helped him lock up, not knowing that the city was going to be in flames moments later, and his store ransacked and emptied of batteries, laundry detergent, beer, and confectionery delights.

The next day, with my older cousin, I ventured to South Park on the East Side of LA where the gangs met up. They were solidifying a temporary peace treaty, joining forces to reckon with the Los Angeles Police Department, their perennial enemy. Not being in a gang, I wasn't privy to their plotting, but, as it turned out, they had already stockpiled weapons from the Western Surplus and pawn shops the night before. They were ready for war. I was mainly at the park to play football. I found teams that contained both the Bloods and Crip gangs, longtime enemies. I've never needed a pass to go to any part of LA—it's my city. I can handle what comes at me from wherever, but I'm beyond the age where I would tempt fate by going into a neighborhood that I know is in a more or less permanent state of war. I also know that danger can visit my doorstep anywhere, and it is with that understanding that I stay vigilante, even when in the hipster-cool kid areas of Silver Lake or Abbot Kinney in Venice.

I was an Afro-Cuban who had survived the hyper violent 80's and 90's without joining a gang or being one of their victims. But just because I wasn't on Florence and Normandie in South Central Los Angeles—I was on chic Beverly Boulevard—didn't mean I was free from harm once the mob mentality took over.

*

The Opie-look alike meant to get the crowd going, so I knew that it was best to eliminate the threat. I reversed my car and felt the rear bumper make contact with him. Consulting my mirror, I saw the Opie go airborne. I placed the car in park and hopped out with my knife in hand and headed toward Opie, who was crawling backward on his hands. Then a voice broke the spell: "Bro, just get back in the car, I'll clear a way for you to get out." I looked around and saw a husky framed black guy, no older than 20, outfitted with a backpack that had a fire extinguisher and water bottles hanging from it. He held a bullhorn in one hand and began to bark into it now: "Clear the way. Clear the way so the cars can get out!" I looked around, only to find a stunned crowd had gathered, with several people holding their cameras trained on me, the shirtless guy wearing flip-flops, knife in hand.

I shifted my sights back to Opie and allowed myself a devilish grin as he limped away with the support of a few girls. I got in the car and inched through the path that the black guy had cleared for me; the insults kept coming from the rowdy crowd.

Once out of the mess, the black guy leaned into my passenger side window and in a hectic voice, as if he was gassed from running a marathon, said: "I'm glad you made it out safely." Looking at my knife that was still in hand, I told him, "I was going to make it out, I wasn't worried about that." I extended my free hand, and we shook. "Some people forgot what this is all about," were his parting words.

In the days that followed, I watched as friends and colleagues from various walks of life expressed their solidarity with the slogan, Black Lives Matter. On social media, many posted photos of themselves at the marches and some fell into the monkey-see-monkey-do trap of posting black squares on the prescribed day. The hashtags and posts never let up. One person I know said, "It's not on black people to change, it's on us white folks." When I said, "you don't owe me shit," he was taken aback. "But, since you think it is on you to do something, now what? With what is in your control in the field you work in, what are you going to do?"

He didn't have an answer because he, like many, are not going to do anything that would alter their lives in a significant way. This friend is an executive and has the ability to actually #raisethepercentage as the latest hashtag goes. Whether he will or not is yet to be seen.

In the weeks that followed, the unrelenting memes and post from white women I know had become nausea inducing. They believe that they are fighting the good fight by parroting the claims that blacks are being killed by the police at alarming rates and that America and its institutions are systemically racist, a claim that I believe isn't supported by the evidence.

I decided to test the resolve of one lady that I'd been acquainted with online (let's call her Patty) who had two solid weeks of posts where she blamed everything from black poverty, incarceration, and even fatherless homes on white supremacy.

My inquiries started with simple challenges to Patty's Instagram stories, "Not true…prove it…maybe for those with victim mindsets…" and eventually we had an exchange that lasted for days. Patty's airing of grievances slowed as LA's protesting winded down and then I saw Patty post that she was enjoying an excursion to the WASP haven of Martha's Vineyard. I couldn't resist a jab and asked Patty if she had taken any of the downtrodden black kids with her, you know a little get-out-of-the-hood experience for those that she has been fighting for with her post. That enraged Patty.

For the next two days our exchange centered on me trying to get Patty to understand that the black community's' problems are not for anyone else to solve, as the root of it starts with fatherless homes. In defense of my position, I quoted no less than Barack Obama, who in 2008 said, "Kids raised without fathers are 5 times more likely to be poor…9 times more likely to drop out…20 times more likely to end up in jail." Patty fell back on her go-to: "Blacks get profiled and get harsher sentences than whites; Blacks don't have good teachers in school…the cops go at them…the system is founded on white supremacy…" She ignored my rebuttals and refused to provide any source for her claims beyond anecdotal cases that made her news feed. I then told Patty, "Seven thousand black men were killed by other black men last year. Does racism account for those deaths too?" Her only answer was white supremacy perpetrated by white men.

I concluded that Patty wasn't really for black people, but that she had instead taken up the popular rhetoric of blaming white men, or "the patriarchy" even for things that were the sole responsibility of the individual. I again invoked Obama's statistics and my own assessment: "Because of the breakdown of the patriarchy, we have the problems in the black community…Getting rid of the patriarch, the father, will lead to more kids dropping out of school, being poor and ending up in the system." Patty didn't want to hear my opinion and ended the exchange as she headed out for drinks with friends while posting the next Black Lives Matter meme of the day.

I stopped short of telling Patty about my conversations with guys I know, ex- and current gang members who are veterans of the LA Riots of 92' street wars and countless prison riots. In so many words, all of them made it clear to me that, "This is a white chick riot using black grievances. They're lucky we didn't get involved."

Patty wouldn't have believed me, but the white, liberal, mostly millennial mob that surrounded my car that day, and that have been protesting nightly in Portland for going on 50 days, those who want to "defund" or "abolish" the police—every one of them would be demanding a police response had actual street guys gotten involved.

I suppose Black lives and Black voices only matter if one is killed by a white cop and I get to blame white supremacy for where I am in life.

Today, I could probably use my own blackness to secure a writing position somewhere, but if I did it that way, I'd always feel like a token, a fraud, someone who couldn't hack it on his own. I'm sure some executive will think he's leveling the playing field, but I'd always feel it was extortion. I'll instead advocate for equality of access; After all, I still have to answer to my conscience at the end of the day. I wonder if Opie is still mending his wounds, or if he's flaunting them as battle scars in the service of Racial Justice.

AVISO! SIN AVISO!

In the second instalment of the Godfather trilogy, Michael Corleone initiates the plot of having Hyman Roth assassinated. Michaels adopted brother and Consigliere, Tom Hagen makes his objections known, prompting Michael to remind Tom that "…if anything in this life is certain, if history has taught us anything, it is that you can kill anyone." Michael then turns to Rocco who states that the mission is 'Difficult, not impossible." Upon Hyman Roth's arrival at the airport under the eye of federal agents, Rocco, posing as a reporter, steps forward, handgun ready and unloads a death shot to Roth. Rocco would be shot dead seconds later as he attempted to escape the scene. Rocco's actions served to lend credence to Michael's prophetic words that you can kill anyone. Sacrificing his life for the organization that he pledged allegiance to also showed that assassin's belief in a cause is greater than their regard for life, even theirs.

Murder has been perpetrated throughout history to varying degrees at the hands of agents of the government and those seeking to overthrow the system that no longer serves their interest. Unlike a mercenary whose allegiance to an army is facilitated through commercial transactions, the actions of an assassin, even when perpetrated by someone with diminished capacity most often are tied to and advance political agendas. An attempt or a successful operation may eliminate a political opponent which often helps in regime change. The means and effectiveness of an assassin's work is often meant to have lasting psychologic effects that strike at the conscious of the target's value system, serving as a warning to the targets group that the opposition is a formidable force to be reckoned with.

In the world of gangs, assassins are no exception as the violence that they perpetrate in society and behind prison walls have their marching orders from their leaders in the various Mexican cartels, with the goal of their violence furthering their monopolization of the international drug trade.

On May 22nd, 2006, in a maximum-security housing unit at Corcoran Prison, a 24yr old inmate Lawrence Alvarado of Los Angeles was shot dead by an officer. The officer's decision to shoot was in response to Alvarado and his confederate, a 26yr old inmate Jose Garcia who were attacking Richard Acosta with inmate made knives.

Inside of prison, an order to eliminate an individual who has lost the political battle comes from a shot caller that serves as the executive officer for the Mexican Mafia. The shot caller and his administration are responsible for collection of fees for contraband that a Mexican inmate introduces to the prison yard and remitting payments to higher ups that often are confined in the Secured Housing Units. Remittance may travel through several carriers in free society as it makes its way to accounts for the Mexican Mafia's leadership, then through another set of hands before it reaches the Mexican cartels that maintain the supply of product.

The executive officers have mandates to contribute a set amount regardless of the realities on the ground. Lockdowns due to assaults may slow their money-making schemes but the executives must meet their monthly quota or face a counsel that could vote to have them removed - a situation that surely is taxing to the conscious.

On the morning of May 22nd, a 28yr old Richard Acosta found out that the dedication of his assassin to carry out their mission was a matter of life or death for them. If Alvarado or Garcia would've declined the orders, they would've been marked for death. Their regard for their image and their adherence to the rules of the organization was more important than their life as Alvarado and Garcia continued to stab Acosta after the tower officer fired two shots of a less-than-lethal projectile weapon. Their attempt to complete their mandate to eliminate Acosta prompted the tower officer to fire one shot from his Mini-14 rifle, killing Alvarado in the process. With disregard for his life and his lifeless comrade who laid next to him, Garcia, continued the mission and stabbed Acosta.

The arrival of officers to the attack saved Garcia and Acosta: Acosta was saved because the officers turned their batons onto Garcia; Garcia was saved because the tower officer could not risk hitting an officer if he fired a shot at Garcia.

Inmate Garcia was serving a sentence of 100yrs to life and Alvarado was sentenced to 40yrs to life. Neither inmate entered Corcoran prison thinking that they would ever see the free world alive, as it stands, an inmate with Mexican Mafia association would be called up at some point to carry out an assassination like the one that they perpetrated. A refusal would be a death sentence and in the case of Garcia, getting caught for the attempted assassination would relegate him to the Special Housing Unit with other Mexican Mafia members and if he managed to live to see a parole date that was 40yrs in the future, he would most certainly be denied because of his continued association and participation in violent acts that is a part of the political campaign that the Mexican Mafia is waging in the California prison system.

The threat of violence by Mexican Mafia soldiers on both sides of the prison walls serves as psychological warfare that is meant to keep the street gangs aligned with their goal of supremacy in the drug trade. The decision makers in the Mexican Mafia understand that assassination of a gang member serves as indirect aggression, ultimately lowering the morale until individuals organize under their flag, adopting their belief system as theirs at the cost of their identity, leaving only an obedient soldier.

In the case of Richard Acosta who was serving a 17yr sentence, his crime was that he questioned the executive officer's rule that Mexican inmates make an increased contribution to make up for a slow month of earnings. Acosta had a steady supply of drugs being mulled in from an enterprising officer and was accustomed to the standard 1/3 contribution, but upon questioning – not refusing the increase – he was marked for death.

The prescribed manner for the executive officer to gain approval to eliminate an inmate would happen with a request being delivered to his handler in the Secured Housing Unit, a process that could be completed in a week and typically facilitated with a phone call from the executive to a contact in free society who would send the request with a visitor who would deliver the message in coded sign language with a decision maker through the glassed visiting booth. Requests of this nature are rarely refused as the decision makers allow latitude for executive officers to carry out attacks to keep the citizenry in line. The added information that eliminating the individual would mean that an inmate who was more aligned with the organization's survival would be given Acosta's drug mule connection and serve to reassure the decision makers that their money-making schemes would continue – minus Acosta.

FIN
Really, that is it. Finito! The End!

Acknowledgements

Many thanks to Jennifer Morgen and Laura Morand. As I wrote each story they served as my audience and first line editors probing me on the stories and characters which often caused me to adjust points so that the next reader would have the clarity that I hope plays out on the page. Margara De La Cruz tear-filled response to reading Jose Marti let me know that I had captured the despair that is familiar with the Cuban community as she has heard over the years the many tales of family, including her mother and father, fleeing the island for La Yuma, knowing that they will never return. Peter Conti for his editorial guidance. Jim Acheson for always taking a moment to read, even while producing Godfather of Harlem in the midst of a global pandemic. The late Paul Eckstein, who co-created Godfather of Harlem. I'd send a text to Paul, to nudge him to check his email as I had shared with him another story and in return, I'd receive a 'thumbs up' emoji or a simple response, "right on…keep it coming." I ran into Paul while driving through Venice, Calif., after several months of scant text exchanges and he told me to stop by his home. Once we were seated in his yard, catching up on our individual projects, I filled him in on the television shows that I had been up for writing assignments on and the frustration with getting in a writing room. He let me know that the line I'm in at the moment is long and filled with people that are just as talented or connected. Once I get to the front of the line and into the room, I will see that there is another line. I will make my way up that line and realize that there is yet another line. Paul always gave me his time. No better gift than a person giving you, their time.

In early 2022 there was a new show on the air about the inmate firefighting program that the California Department of Corrections has had going on for many years. I read the trades daily and hoped that I would get a chance to lend my expertise in the area of fire safety and being an inmate. While I was incarcerated, I participated in the program. Surely, I would be a fit. After a great meeting with Asher Landay and Chelsea Sabella at Jerry Bruckheimer television, the production company behind the show, I was then sent onto a meeting with the co-creator and showrunner of what was already shaping up to be the breakout hit show for CBS, Fire Country. Joan Rater and Tia Napolitano had read my work and listened to my ideas. Jim Acheson and Rob Weiss sent recommendation emails to the decision makers with the hope that their words would put me in a better position. Fingers and eyes were crossed for luck. Going into shabbat and being told that a decision may come the following week, my caller i.d. read Agency for The Performing Arts (APA). Jack Leighton, Danny Alexander and Joe Fronk (aka, The Dream Team) called me on a conference line to tell me that I had reached the front of the line and was going to be on the writing staff of Fire Country.

So it began, I had reached the front of the line and was let in the room. Just as Paul had said. I saw that I was in yet another line, but I was in the room.

First day in and Joan Rater had her episode before the room. Joan has worked on many shows that have run for multiple seasons. Fair to say that she had seen it all. There wasn't any ego tripping. The best ideas won, even if they came from an assistant. If it was best for the characters and the story, then it made its way to the screen.

Last day of the writing room, as I was on my way out of the door, after weeks of working on Tia's end of season episode, I read the latest draft and noticed a line from a guest character that had her saying that she was with the "district attorneys office." I mention to Tia that the character should be stating that she is with the "State Attorneys Office of Investigations." Two separate entities. The average viewer wouldn't pay much attention to the government entity name as it was not a part of the show on a regular basis. When I read the updated version of the script that night, I saw that Tia had corrected the line to reflect my note. No big ego trips. It was what was best for the character and the story.

Many thanks to Asher, Chelsea, Tia, Joan, David Gould and all at Fire Country that made my first television writing experience a blast. Your time and experience is appreciated. I look forward to debating ideas all the way up to season 20.

I hope that Jose Marti's, versos sencillos and the other shorts were worthy of the time that you invested. All I did was translate simple words into simple sentences with the goal of a story coming out, worthy of a second, third and if I am lucky, a fourth thumbing of the pages.

Riley Perez

Made in the USA
Las Vegas, NV
30 July 2023

75413218R00075